D0894974

83

Marcus and Narcissa Whitman
PIONEERS OF OREGON

ALSO BY JAMES DAUGHERTY

MARCUS AND NARCISSA WHITMAN

Pioneers of Oregon

STORY AND PICTURES BY

JAMES DAUGHERTY

NEW YORK

The Viking Press

1954

Sharples

To my mother,

whose courage and humor shone brightest

when the going was toughest

CONTENTS

7

PART ONE
THE WESTERN STAR
On the Trail to Oregon

INVITATION

Pardner, bridle your piebald pony
While I tighten the girth on this wall-eyed cayuse.
Have you your Hawken rifle stocked to the muzzle?
Your scalping knife and your trap bags? Your Navajo blanket all rolled?
Do not delay a moment; today we ride west beyond the Missouri.

Take a squint there to the far horizon, my bold compañero,
Where the rolling prairie and the far sky meet.
Those rivers, plains, mountains, all are yours.
Help yourself, there are no fences beyond the Big Muddy.
It's all yours; sign no papers; I ask no commission;
We mention no real-estate deals beyond the Missouri.

What if you do not arrive at the station tomorrow
At eight-fifteen? The commuters will not long miss you.
Come with me, amigo, along the river bluffs,
Splashing through the shallows across the Platte.
Yonder gleam white the walls of Fort Laramie.
Let us follow the Sweetwater up through South Pass to where the waters
*   flow westward.*

Old Hickory and the De Witt Clinton

The people from over the mountains had won. General "Old Hickory" Andrew Jackson was president. The New England aristocrats had been turned out. The buckskin hunters of Kentucky, the Tennessee coon hunters, the Illinois farmers, the Tarheels, the Buckeyes, the roaring Ohio flatboat men had taken over the government. Let the people rule.

There were to be no more New England or Virginia dynasties of tidewater aristocrats. America extended from the Atlantic to the Mississippi, and the frontier farmers and backwoodsmen had come into their own. Jackson was their man. He and the Kentucky hunters had licked the redcoats at "Noo Orleens." The ringtailed roarers and the

11

gamecocks of the wilderness had put their man in the president's mansion, and now he was going to roar.

There were other strange doings. Up in Albany on August 9, 1831, a contraption called a steam locomotive had hauled three stagecoaches loaded with passengers for seventeen miles on rails to Schenectady. Spouting smoke and fire, the *De Witt Clinton,* as the engine was called, had reached the terrific speed of thirty miles an hour. Fiery sparks had burned holes in the clothes of the passengers; even their umbrellas had failed to protect them from the fiery rain. At one point the passengers had got out and wedged fence rails between the coaches to keep them from bumping and jerking the lights out of riders. Everybody knew that, what with the new turnpikes and fine canals, such newfangled contraptions would never amount to much.

True, steamboats had been plowing between Pittsburgh and New Orleans for some years, and a steamboat called the *Yellowstone* had even gone up the Missouri as far as her namesake river. In time news of all these doings got circulated through the country by the little local newspapers, and there was plenty to jaw about around the stoves in the general stores where at least once a week everybody in the neighborhood dropped in.

By 1830 western New York was populous, with small towns, decent Christian communities with churches, free schools, newspapers, and politics, all hand-fashioned by the sons and daughters and grandchildren of men who had fought at Concord, Trenton, and Yorktown.

AROUND THE POT-BELLIED STOVE
PRATTSBURG, NEW YORK, 1835

The kettle purred busily on the pot-bellied stove in the back of the general store. The glowing stove threw out a genial warmth, and the pleasant smells of woodsmoke, tobacco, and ground coffee greeted the red noses of the customers as they stomped in from the white February outdoors.

Lounging about the stove were the usual town characters. Greetings, banter, and bits of gossip passed pleasantly back and forth as familiar figures came and went.

The main subject of talk was Judge Prentiss's daughter and her coming marriage with the doctor who had appeared so dramatically from the Far West.

"We allus figgered around this town that if a girl wasn't married time she was twenty-seven she never would be," drawled a man with gray chin-whiskers.

"Guess a good-lookin' girl like Narcissa Prentiss had plenty of offers. Seems like none of the yokels around here was ever good enough for her though," responded a lounger.

"That young feller Hank Spalding, he kept after her hardest of 'em all. It shore broke him up when he knew she really wouldn't have him. They was both goin' to the Franklin Academy at the time. He left school and went off somewheres. They say he was so broke up he got religion, joined the church, and got to be a first-rate preacher."

"Well, to my way of thinking, a smart girl like her is plumb crazy to think of marrying a harum-scarum doctor and go a-missionaryin' off to Oregon for to get scalped by them wild Injuns," added a customer in a green bonnet. "Seems like some people these days would do most anything to get a lot of attention and notoriety," she added scornfully.

At this the kettle gave an indignant snort of steam. A red-bearded man brought his chair down on the floor, knocked the ashes from his corncob pipe, opened the stove door, and threw in a birch log. Sleigh bells jangled outside, the door slammed behind a new customer, and a clamor of greetings and banter again went around the stove.

Narcissa Prentiss was one of the smartest girls in that part of New York State, and one of the best-looking too, with her red-gold hair and her gray-blue eyes. She had had a better education than most women in the western part of the state, having gone to Miss Willard's Female Seminary at Troy and graduated from the Franklin Academy at Prattsburg. She and her sister Jane had enterprisingly conducted an infants' school and organized ladies' prayer meetings. Narcissa had a fine contralto voice and loved to sing. She was a vital sort of person who had ideas and did something about them.

The Prentiss family were of Puritan New England stock. Judge Prentiss and his wife had brought up a family of nine girls and boys to be as fine a lot of young Americans as you would find anywhere in the country. Like most good Presbyterians and Congregationalists, the Prentisses subscribed to and read the *Missionary Herald*. Narcissa always watched for its arrival because it contained news about the missionaries who went to foreign lands to teach and convert the heathen. When she was sixteen she made up her mind "to consecrate myself without reserve to the Missionary work waiting the leadings of Providence concerning me." Narcissa was growing up to be a very pious, patient, and determined young lady.

THE A. B. C. F. M.

Church members throughout the States knew that the letters A. B. C. F. M. stood for "American Board of Commissioners for Foreign Missions." The American Board had been having its difficulties ever since a stirring story had appeared in the *Christian Advocate*. Four Nez Percé Indians had come to St. Louis from beyond the Rockies. They said they had come to learn about the white man's God. They asked that they might take the white man's Book of Heaven—the Bible—back to their people.

"When I tell my poor blind people, after one more snow, in the big council, that I did not bring the Book, no word will be spoken by our old men or by our young braves. One by one they will rise up and go out in silence. My people will die in darkness, and they will go on the long path to the other hunting grounds. No white man will go with them, and no white man's Book will make the way plain. I have no more words." These were the words of The Rabbit-Skin Leggings as reported in the *Christian Advocate* for March 1833. And all good churchgoers read them and said it was a shame that the "Wise Men from the West" had gone back without the Bible. But no one seemed eager to go with them across the Great American Desert and teach them Christianity.

There were, however, three New England ministers.

Reverend Samuel Parker, Mr. Allis, and Mr. Dunbar, who offered to go. They made a dash to St. Louis to catch the annual fur traders' caravan starting west to the mountains but arrived too late. Allis and Dunbar went on to the Pawnees on the Missouri and began missions among them. Dr. Parker came back to Ithaca, New York, determined to rouse the people to support the great work of a mission to the Indians beyond the Rocky Mountains. Among the interested but not very eager listeners he found two sincere young people who were deeply in earnest about helping. One was Dr. Marcus Whitman. As a boy he had wanted to study for the ministry but had not had the means to get schooling and so had studied the more practical profession of medicine. He had graduated and been in practice some eight years. He was also a good farmer and a practical Christian.

Dr. Parker's other young friend was Narcissa Prentiss. She had had experience as a teacher and was eager, devoted, and competent. Together these three discussed practical ways to take Christianity across the wilderness to the Indians.

It was finally worked out with the American Board that Parker and Whitman would be sent to the Rocky Mountains to meet with the Nez Percés and to determine whether the Indians would really accept Christian teachers and a permanent mission in their midst. After thorough investigation the two men would return and report to the Board. This journey might take over a year.

Narcissa was eager to go with them, but Dr. Parker wisely counseled her to wait. If, when they returned, the Board should authorize a mission and call for volunteers,

she could then offer to go. As the three planned the Indian
mission together, Narcissa and Marcus Whitman had soon
found that they were in love. More than this, they were
dedicated to the same great missionary cause. Quietly they
decided that they would share this great adventure as man
and wife.

There was no time for a long romantic courtship. Already Marcus and Dr. Parker were planning their journey
across the desert and mountains. Narcissa would be lonely
and anxious, waiting for Marcus to return from the long
and dangerous expedition, but it now seemed possible that
her dream might actually come true.

That spring of 1835, Dr. Parker and Marcus Whitman
joined the American Fur Company caravan at Council
Bluffs under the famous partisan Lucien Fontenelle and
crossed the prairies and mountains to the rendezvous on
the Green River. Here they talked with the Nez Percé
chiefs. There was no doubt that the Indians wanted to be
taught Christianity. There were souls to be saved and no
time to lose. It was decided that Whitman should return
to the States with Thomas Fitzpatrick and the fur caravan
and organize a mission to Oregon. Parker would go on
alone to the Pacific to gather information and explore for
mission sites.

The Reverend Samuel Parker was not a young man, but
he rode westward into the mountains with a serene assur-
ance that the God who had guided him through the fifty-
six years of his earthly journey was with him on this
mission to bring Christ to the benighted children of darkness. For a few days he was accompanied by Jim Bridger
and his brigade of mountain veterans. They did not go

much for religion, but the kindness and courage of this saintly man had won their respect by the time they parted.

Parker rode on with the Nez Percés toward the Columbia. As they journeyed through a fantastic world of savage peaks and gloomy canyons the Indians listened to his teaching of the God of love, feeling the greatness of the man's nature rather than understanding the interpreter's words. Under the dark mountain firs and by the still lakes this Christian pioneer preached Christ's doctrine to the eager ears of the savage listeners. Even in pious New England his parishioners had never wakened him in the night to hear more about the immortality of the soul. An exalted happiness filled his devoted spirit. He had a sincere affection for these people, and, more than anyone who came after, he understood and respected the dignity and spiritual impulses of the Indian.

When he was stricken with illness on the wild trail they tenderly cared for him and brought him safely to the British fort at Walla Walla and the healing hospitality of Mr. Pambrun, the factor. When he recovered he continued down the Columbia to Fort Vancouver, where he preached and taught for a time. Then he took a ship for Hawaii and finally sailed back to the States. After his return home he wrote a book, *Journal of an Exploring Tour beyond the Rocky Mountains*. It was full of understanding of the strange people, white and red, among whom he had sojourned, and it was one of the first and best guides to Oregon.

Whitman sadly parted from his companion. As he rode eastward with the returning caravan his thoughts were aflame with visions of a great mission. His whole life was changing and being brought into focus. He was now a dedicated man. And there was Narcissa. He thought how she would thrill to this new prospect, which would fulfill all her dreams of becoming a missionary to the Indians. They were to share the great adventure together.

THE VOLUNTEER

In Boston, Secretary Greene of the American Board opened the morning mail in his office. One letter was especially interesting. He read:

Amity
Feb. 23, 1835.

To the Secretaries of the A. B. C. F. M.
Dear Brethren:

Permit an unworthy sister to address you. Having obtained favor of the Lord and desiring to live for the conversion of the world, I now offer myself to the American Board to be employed in their service among the heathen, if counted worthy.

The letter ended:

I frequently desired to go to the heathen but only half-heartedly—and it was not until the first Monday in January 1824 that I felt to consecrate myself without reserve to the Missionary work waiting the leadings of Providence concerning me.

Feeling it more my privilege than duty to labor for the conversion of the heathen, I respectfully submit myself to your direction.

Your unworthy sister in the Lord,
Narcissa Prentiss

Several recommendations of the applicant from ministers accompanied this letter. A postscript to one of them said, "As it is probable that Miss Prentiss will hereafter become the companion of Doct. Marcus Whitman (should he be established missionary beyond the Rocky Mts.) it may be proper to add that he expressed a desire that she might accompany us on our mission."

Mr. Greene thoughtfully reread the letter. Here was the answer to the call of the heathen and to the dilemma of the American Board that had been so perplexing. A Christian doctor and farmer and a dedicated teacher were offering to go, as man and wife, to take the Book of Heaven to the "Wise Men from the West."

THE INTRUDER
RUSHVILLE, NEW YORK, DECEMBER 1835

In Rushville, New York, Sunday came around as usual after six hard working days. It was bright and clear, and the sun shone dazzlingly on the snow. It was so still that it seemed as though nothing had ever moved since the beginning of time.

At precisely half-past ten the church bell chimed clear and sweet. The tune and the words of the hymn were inseparable to all who heard: "Peace be to this congregation, peace to every heart therein."

Exactly fifteen minutes later dignified men in broadcloth and beaver hats, with marvelously upholstered ladies holding their arms, came out of prim houses. Behind them marched, two abreast, children of varied ages and sizes, laundered to an unbelievable cleanliness. Little family processions converged on the white church.

At five minutes to eleven all the pews but the first three were filled to the aisles. The organ tones vibrated solemnly in crescendo. Each member of the congregation was in his appointed place. An air of holy expectancy settled upon the congregation and overflowed into the vestibule.

Suddenly three strange apparitions stalked swiftly down the center aisle and sat conspicuously in the front row. The dark impassive faces and straight black hair of the two boys plainly showed them to be Indians. The shaggy man who sat between them seemed unaccountably familiar, except that he was arrayed in a buffalo overcoat and buckskin jacket. His broad strong face was sun-browned. His dark hair was oddly streaked with gray. It was a face that had once been familiar in Rushville.

A whisper ran through the congregation. "Why, it's Marcus Whitman!"

He had come back from the Rockies a whole year ahead of schedule, bringing stirring news from the Nez Percés. The Indians were ready and eager for the Christian teachers. There was no need to wait. Marcus had returned at once, and Parker had gone on to the Columbia to prepare the way for the Christian mission.

Marcus spoke in churches and halls to large audiences eager to hear his story. He had found it was true that beyond the Rocky Mountains hundreds of the heathen Indians were calling for the Gospel, and thousands of benighted souls were waiting to be saved. But who would go or contribute dollars for this great purpose? Christians

wept for the poor benighted Indians, but no one offered to
go, and there were few dollars.

There were evenings in the Prentiss home when Whitman sat with the family around the fire and told stories of
hardship and adventure on the long trail across the plains.

When he and Parker had reached the Fur Company
brigade on the Missouri the mountain men had been hostile. They had no use for preachers. They had even thrown
things at them. Then the plague had come up the Missouri.
Cholera struck. Men were dying. Day and night the doctor
watched by bedsides, tended and nursed and brought men
back from the last rendezvous. There were no more insults
flung at the missionaries. From then on the parson and the
doctor were members of the brotherhood of the mountains.
Soon these two greenhorns were sharing the wild wayfaring like seasoned mountain men.

At the rendezvous Jim Bridger—"Old Gabe," as the
trappers called him—had come to the doctor for a favor.
There was a Blackfoot arrowhead in his back; it had been
floating around in his system for several years, and it kind
of itched him lately. Would the doctor butcher it out for
him? Deftly the doctor probed and cut while the Indians
stood around and admired. They were specialists in torture, and they closely watched Old Gabe's face as he
calmly puffed at his pipe. The doctor held up the three-inch
arrowhead in his bloody fingers. The iron barb was passed
around with grunts of approval. Other mountain men
asked to have the hardware removed from their carcasses,
and the doctor performed other deft operations. Everything depended on the good will of the mountain men, and
Marcus had won it.

A WEDDING AND A DEPARTURE
ANGELICA, NEW YORK, FEBRUARY 18, 1836

"Yes, you might argue that it could be done, that it was possible for Americans to cross overland to Oregon. There were Lewis and Clark, Hunt and the Astorians, and Mr. Wyeth the Boston iceman, but nothing has come of it and never will. People who talk about going to live in Oregon are plumb crazy." This is the way people talked in the frontier towns of western New York.

But Marcus Whitman knew better. He was a practical man, and he had crossed the mountains and come back. He purposed to go again, and he was sure that women and wagons could be taken to Oregon.

Narcissa's faith told her that this was God's work and that He would prosper it. She came of a people who relied on Christian prayer and had proved its power. She and Marcus were going to Oregon together to take God's word to the heathen.

They had been in love almost from their first meeting. But there was something more; they stood shoulder to shoulder as crusaders and comrades in a great and holy cause. They were of a people who had pushed westward across ocean and wilderness, with their faith and their Bibles, seeking freedom and light, and they had never stopped nor turned back.

These two were starting again on the western trail, following the star, as their fathers and mothers had before them. They were planning to begin a new life in an utterly strange world. They would leave behind them all the old sureties and comforts, the prospects of material success, civilized society, dear companionships, and family ties. It was a future that held no prospects of material gain, only hardship, danger, perhaps tragedy. But they were sure in their faith, eager, dedicated, and confident. On this stern path ahead they would never doubt, never regret, never turn back.

That February Sunday afternoon in the crowded church in Angelica, New York, was hushed and solemn. Strangely, Narcissa and her family had come dressed in black. As the congregation joined in the final hymn women were weeping and men's voices choked with emotion. In the last verses only Narcissa's voice rose sweet and clear to the end.

It was on March 3 that the Whitmans left Prattsburg. There were tender farewells. All knew that this parting was for years, perhaps forever. But the ties of the old affections and memories would outlast space and the years. The sleigh drove off with a jingle of bells, a fluttering of scarfs, and calls of "Farewell" and "God bless you till we meet again." As they reached the crest of the hill Narcissa looked back for the last time at the white church on the hill and the familiar houses across the snowy landscape. She turned away, wiping the tears from her face, and leaned her head against Marcus's comforting shoulder.

DOWN THE OHIO

Pittsburgh stood on the point of land where the Allegheny and Monongahela Rivers, flowing north and south, join to form the Ohio. It was a grim gray place of coal and iron, of fire and smoke. In its blast furnaces was the white-hot ore that would make the metal bones of the expanding republic. Along its waterfront were clustered the varied river craft of the Ohio—skiffs, rafts, barges, arks, broadhorns, and, towering over all, the black stacks of white steamboats. The crews that manned these craft were the roaring river men, the godless half-horse half-alligator bullies of the river, who bawled that they could outfight, outrun, outshoot, outspit, and outcuss any man alive.

Here Marcus engaged passage to Cincinnati for his party on the steamboat *Siam*. Besides Narcissa there were the two Nez Percé boys, called Richard and John; Miss Emeline Palmer, who was going to meet and marry her fiancé Samuel Allis, now a missionary among the Pawnee Indians, and young Dr. Satterlee and his wife, who was ill with a very bad cough. These last were going as missionaries to the Pawnees.

The *Siam* was a raftlike hull propelled by steam-driven paddlewheels. Her high black stacks belched forth smoke clouds and fiery cinders as the Negro firemen stoked her furnaces with green pine logs. But her staterooms were gaudy with gilding and her railings and decks fancy with scrollwork. Her whistle screamed, bells jangled, the great paddlewheels slowly churned as she made headway into the boiling current.

The river swept in great bends around the shaggy shoulders of the Appalachians. She was on the rampage from the spring floods that emptied in angry torrents from the rivers that poured down the great valley. The *Siam* stopped at raw settlements where pioneering families debarked with their tools and belongings and plunged into the tall timber to make homes and farms in the new land. An endless stream of lanky, muscular movers was pouring down the river to strip the forests of the valley and to raise corn and wheat, cattle and hogs, cabins and towns, in the heartland of the Middle West.

From the hurricane deck of the *Siam,* Marcus and Narcissa watched the moon rise over hills tender with spring green and touch the river mist with enchantment.

CINCINNATI

Cincinnati was barely keeping her skirts dry above the high-water mark of the spring floods. Along the levees all the products of a fat land—corn, pork, whisky, hides— were being shipped aboard the motley river craft for the downstream trade clear to New Orleans. The city was the metropolis of the Middle West. Here the slave South and the free North met, shook hands, traded, bartered, and argued. It was a city of wealth and pride, schools and churches, of young culture and hearty manners.

As the Whitman party came down the gangplank a rugged figure strode out of the melee, waving a huge beaver hat. It was the Reverend Henry Harmon Spalding. Baldish and bearded, with a glittering eye, he was a robust and dominant figure who radiated piety and importance.

There were cordial greetings and introductions. As Narcissa and Spalding shook hands she noted a gleam in his cold eyes. Did he still resent her rejection of long ago?

He introduced Mrs. Spalding—"Sister Eliza," as she was called. She seemed demure and reserved in the shadow of her aggressive husband, groping cautiously for friend- ship. The two women talked guardedly, taking in sharp first impressions. Eliza was dark and sallow, seemed melancholy, ailing, nursing her own soul, a contrast to Narcissa's blondness and healthy exuberance.

Marcus and Spalding plunged into the details of the expedition. The Reverend David Greene's letters had arrived, giving the Board's instructions for equipment, schedules, transportation, and conduct. Proudly Spalding showed his wagon. He had built it himself and driven it west from New York State. It was strongly made, but, like Mr. Spalding's nature, it was without springs. Marcus was fascinated with it. He examined it lovingly and in detail. His dream of taking a wagon to Oregon was about to become a reality.

Cincinnati was full of sin and religion. There were churches—Baptist, Congregationalist, Methodist, Catholic, Quaker. The visiting mission attended all of them. They heard the famous Dr. Lyman Beecher preach to his enraptured congregation. Narcissa talked with his daughter Harriet. She was an ardent Abolitionist and told stories of how Christians, and especially the Quakers, helped escaping slaves to freedom in the North on the "underground railroad." The two women were both crusaders, aflame to save souls. Narcissa learned that the Ohio was a river that separated the darkness and the light; it lay between Egyptian slavery and the promised land of freedom.

Marcus himself superintended the installing of the precious wagon aboard the St. Louis boat, on which the mission was now to proceed. At St. Louis, Whitman would arrange with the American Fur Company for the party to join the fur caravan to the mountains. Only with the caravan's protection was it possible safely to cross the Indian-infested wilderness.

The passengers aboard the St. Louis boat were now sanctified by the presence of the Reverend Mr. Spalding and his wife. He was a man powerful in audible prayer, especially when he had a large audience, and his sermons terrified sinners and depressed saints. A chilly sanctity elevated him above the genial humanities of the rest of the passengers. But he had the awesome accomplishments of a popular revivalist minister and was highly respected by all.

However, underneath all this, Narcissa sensed the snarling enmity to her happiness, and Marcus controlled with difficulty his anger at the man's malice toward his young wife.

But above all this they were Christians bound together in the service of a great cause. Besides, Marcus and Narcissa were too happy, their cup was too full, the song too sweet, for resentment or anger to endure.

They were now out on the mighty Mississippi, headed upstream. A very serious question must be decided. Should they travel on the Sabbath? Was it breaking the Fourth Commandment to do so? Mr. Spalding thought so. The Board had especially instructed them to keep the Sabbath. Their religion demanded it. At the next landing the mission party left the boat, debarked on the Illinois shore, and spent a peaceful Sabbath in prayer, Bible-reading, and listening to Mr. Spalding's sermon. Fortunately they caught an upriver steamer on Monday and were soon at the swarming levee of St. Louis.

ST. LOUIS

"Why, it's Whitman," shouted Fitzpatrick, leaping up from his desk. "Doc, you old coon, it's great to be seeing you here again!" he added, giving Marcus a staggering wallop between his broad shoulders.

"Well, you're a sight for sore eyes, you old hornswoggling coyote, you," whooped Marcus, giving the tall Scotsman a terrific dig in the ribs.

Marcus had first met Thomas Fitzpatrick at Fort William the year before, and the famous mountain partisan had taken the brigade with the two missionaries on through the South Pass to the rendezvous at Horse Creek in the Green River Valley, Wyoming.

After this formal Missouri greeting, the two men sat down and were soon deep in the arrangements for the Whitman mission to join the caravan at Council Bluffs, several hundred miles up the Missouri. From here the expedition would shove off on the thousand-mile trek across the plains to the Green River rendezvous beyond the Rockies.

As Narcissa ventured on the streets of St. Louis she saw for the first time shaggy mountain men and painted Indian chiefs, French voyageurs, Canadian pork-eaters, and proud Spanish gentlemen. She heard a strange babble of tongues, Scotch and Irish brogues, Negro laughter, and the drawling Missouri dialect. It was like a fantastic carnival, a costume ball of people from the farthest frontiers of the continent. On this westward wayfaring each day brought new and fascinating pictures of America to the eager young lady from New York State.

The mission party left St. Louis for Liberty, Missouri, on the steamboat *Chariton*. The other passengers and crew were the rough and savage men of the frontier. The Spaldings kept to themselves, shunning the godless men who swore, drank, and gambled as they lolled about the decks. For Narcissa this novel scene was full of interest. After the first day, which was enlivened by fist fights among the crew to determine who should be the leader, things were quieter. In the pilothouse she watched the captain and the pilot outsmart Old Man Missouri and all his tricks of snags, sawyers, sandbars, and the shifting boiling current in spring flood.

At the frontier town of Liberty, three hundred miles up the Missouri, the party left the *Chariton*, which went no farther. The settlement was a cluster of cabins, a store, and a saloon, in a sea of mud, raw and bleak in the chill spring wind and rain. Here they were to wait for the company boat that would take them to Council Bluffs, where they would overtake the fur caravan.

Samuel Allis arrived from the Pawnee mission to keep his rendezvous with Emeline Palmer. He was to take her back to the Pawnee mission as his wife. There were bustle and preparation for the marriage ceremony, which Mr. Spalding performed with great solemnity. The women were now busy making a tent for the expedition out of striped bed-ticking. It was gaudy and stylish, designed to shelter ten people when in service on the prairie.

One day a steamer from St. Louis stopped at the landing and deposited an exhausted young man. He was William H. Gray, and he had been desperately trying for weeks to catch up with the mission. The Board had accepted his application to accompany it as lay assistant and mechanic. He was a pious young man and an excellent carpenter. Marcus welcomed him as a valuable addition to their enterprise.

Ten days of anxious waiting passed. At last it was decided that Spalding and Gray should take the wagon, horses, and cattle up the west bank of the Missouri to Council Bluffs to meet the fur caravan. Whitman, Allis, Satterlee, and the women were to wait at Liberty for the boat. The doctor could not leave because of Mrs. Satterlee. The young wife was sinking in the last stages of consumption. In spite of all the doctor could do she died in a few days.

In the little burial ground on the river bank a group of black figures stood among the white crosses. They made a somber silhouette against the dun sky and the gray river. The minister had finished the burial service and closed the Bible. "Let us sing hymn—" A blast from a steamboat whistle drowned out the sentence.

"It's the Company boat! Run for the landing and hail her," cried Marcus.

From the end of the landing pier the men shouted and waved. They could see the steamer come opposite the landing, but she kept on in midstream. "She's not going to stop. She's not going to take us on," wailed Marcus. The steamer plowed on upstream. "No room for any more passengers," came the faint call across the water.

The dejected men walked slowly back to the open grave. The mournful refrain of the hymn died away. The women dropped a few prairie flowers on the coffin. The men filled the grave. Sadly the little procession walked back to the town.

OVERTAKING THE FUR CARAVAN

Whitman now summoned the party to a conference. His plan called for swift action. By fast travel they could overtake Spalding and might still reach the caravan before it started. Marcus purchased saddle horses. Allis bought a wagon, in which they loaded their baggage. They pulled out of Liberty and headed across the prairie toward Fort Leavenworth, where they found that Spalding had left only the day before on the way to the caravan, which was now at the Loup Fork.

The party finally overtook Spalding and Gray beyond the Otoe Agency on the south bank of the Platte some thirty miles west of the Missouri. The first days of hard riding had left Narcissa saddlesore and exhausted. But each morning she had started valiantly, until now she sat easily on her tall horse and could ride all day like a hardened plainsman.

At the Otoe Agency they learned that they had missed the company caravan by four and a half days. They might still overtake them, and Marcus was determined they must.

Their outfit now consisted of fourteen horses, six mules, fifteen cattle—including four milch cows—and two farm wagons. On the prairie they had picked up a sixteen-year-youngster who said he was heading west to become a mountain man. He joined the party and helped Mr. Gray and the two Indian boys drive the herd. The cattle could not keep pace with the horses and dropped behind.

Fording two rivers was a dangerous job and caused delay. "Husband became so completely exhausted with swimming the river on Thursday, May 9th, that it was with difficulty he made the shore the last time," wrote Narcissa anxiously.

As a last chance Whitman rode ahead on a fast horse, overtook the fur train, and begged Fitzpatrick to wait. His friend explained that his timetable was set and included no waits. Marcus rode back and urged his party on for the final spurt. It was one o'clock at night when the exhausted missionaries reached the sleeping caravan. By a superhuman effort the mission had met its first crisis. These greenhorns had passed a rough initiation of hard riding, cattle driving, and river fording.

NARCISSA ON HORSEBACK

The Rocky Mountain Fur Caravan, under its veteran partisan Fitzpatrick, consisted of seventy men, four hundred animals, and seven heavily loaded wagons, each drawn by six Missouri mules. With them, in a two-wheeled cart, Milton Sublette the fur trader, with his wooden leg, was again setting out for the mountains.

When Narcissa and Eliza emerged from the striped bed-ticking tent next morning they found themselves in the center of an awestricken circle of gaping mountain men and amazed Indians, some of whom had never seen a white woman before. Fitzpatrick rode up with a hearty welcome for the newcomers. The partisan was an eye-filling man.

His tight-fitting buckskins were molded to his lean, muscular figure, and the gaunt face under his broad-brimmed hat was fringed with a grizzled beard. He lifted his hat as he took Narcissa's small hand in his horny paw.

"You've given us the honor, ma'am, of being the first brigade ever to take white women over the mountains," he said.

The two mission wagons and cattle took up their place at the end of the long caravan that strung out in a thin line across the green plains. They were soon in a treeless land where the earth and sky met in a shimmering haze of heat. Across the blue void of the sky cloud processions slowly drifted in changing shapes. The eyes of the Easterners were blinded by the burning sun that filled the vast emptiness with a dazzling brightness. As the morning freshness wore off the caravan fell into the monotonous pace that held on till the noon camp and then on again through the hot afternoon till sunset. At night the caravan "forted up" in a hollow square formed on three sides by the baggage; the fourth side was the River Platte. In this enclosure the horses were picketed, while the cattle grazed outside. Each mess of ten men started its fire of buffalo chips. Eliza and Narcissa learned to make a sort of bread out of flour and water baked in the embers of the cookfire. Meals would be meager until they came to the buffalo country. Their table, chairs, and bed were the good prairie earth.

"My health was never better than since I have been on the river. I was weighed last week, and came up to 136 pounds," wrote Narcissa. She took to the rough outdoor life and the hardships of prairie wayfaring with zest and good humor.

The caravan was following the River Platte, which flowed from the Rockies for a thousand miles across the sandy plains to the Missouri. Its shining surface was a mile wide at the Loup Fork, but its shifting channel was too shallow for any craft but venturesome bull boats. It was described as "a thousand miles long and six inches deep." But it was a guide for the fur brigades, which had followed it ever since Ashley's first expedition to the mountains in 1824. Their first objective was Fort William on the Laramie River near where it flowed into the Platte, some six hundred miles from the Missouri. The fort and trading post had been built by the famous fur trader William Sublette in 1834 and bore his first name. It soon became famous under the name of Fort Laramie. It became the great crossroads of the West, where Indians, trappers, emigrants, and traders met, rested, and caroused.

TEA ON THE PRAIRIE

Narcissa was an observant reporter, and she wanted to share the excitement and strangeness of this adventure with her family at home. All her life had been shared in affectionate exuberance with her eight brothers and sisters and her loving parents. Her journal and letters overflowed with a singing gaiety as she recorded all the fascinating details of this new experience. Eliza was moody and sickly, but she stuck on her horse like a hero. "Sister Spalding is very resolute, no shrinking with her. She possesses much fortitude. I like her very much. She wears well upon acquaintance."

Their clothes for this expedition were the conventional

ladies' costume of the time. They were upholstered in yards
of petticoats that trailed in the dirt. They rode, of course,
sidesaddle, their knees desperately clutching the awkward
pommels of ladies' saddles. Narcissa would no more have
ridden astride than she would have ridden naked to church
on Sunday morning in Prattsburg. She rather daringly,
however, wore a pair of gentleman's boots, although to
show a foot was considered unladylike. And like a mountain man, she carried a scalping knife in her belt.

She liked the trappers and drew them out to tell tall tales
of the lost valleys of Absoraka. Her blond beauty dazzled
and haunted lonely men with memories of a world they
had long ago deserted.

She was delighted when Fitzpatrick introduced her to
his friend Captain James Stewart. Stewart was a real Scots
nobleman who had escaped from the boredom of Euro-
pean aristocracy and had been enjoying himself hugely
across the wide Missouri. Narcissa, with true Yankee
deference for the nobility, gave a prairie tea-party in his
honor. They sat in a circle on the ground as Narcissa
passed the tea in tin cups with the luxury of sugar. Captain
Stewart told tales of the far-off Columbia to which they
were going and where he himself had been. At the campfire
that night Narcissa accommodated with a song, and her
clear contralto voice rose in the star-spangled prairie
night.

The Reverend Mr. Spalding warned her against this
familiarity with sinners. The trappers admired her. They
said she had grit and sand and gumption and it was a great
pity she was going to be wasted on the Indians.

The caravan had passed the forks of the Platte and was

now in the buffalo country. This was the land of plenty. There would now be fresh meat daily. The two women imprudently ventured up a high bluff for a first close-up of a great buffalo bull, who stood grazing peacefully. He lifted his great shaggy head, snorted, and made off.

"Not one in our number relishes buffalo meat as well as my husband and I," wrote Narcissa. "He has a different way for cooking every piece of meat. . . . We have meat and tea in the morn, and tea and meat at noon. All our variety consists of the different ways of cooking. I relish it well and it agrees with me. My health is excellent. So long as I have buffalo meat I do not wish anything else. Sister Spalding is affected by it considerably—has been quite sick."

THE FORT

There it was at last! Fort William! Its walls shone in the clear air.

As they came nearer they could see the Indian teepees silhouetted darkly against its high corner bastions. Cannons slept in the tower over the gate; the Indians were fearful of awakening their dreadful thunder. The caravan broke line and came galloping across Laramie River, splashing and whooping, rifles cracking. Inside the double gate the compound was full of excited groups. There were riotous mountain greetings among the trappers and their squaws. Half-breed children and lean Indian dogs swarmed everywhere. The white women were a sensation —they were the first that the fort had ever seen. There was a welcoming dinner with a table and chairs and everyone in high spirits—except Mr. Spalding, who was always depressed by the exuberance of sinners.

In their camp outside the fort, the mission rested and prepared for the mountains. For the first time since Leavenworth the women washed their clothes. The caravan shifted its baggage from the seven wagons to muleback, for wagons were not taken farther west than the fort. One wagon would go on, for Marcus must now prove that wagons and women could be taken across the mountains. The mission held services, and Narcissa led the hymn-singing. The older mountain men shook their heads and said Whitman was plumb crazy to try to take a wagon over the mountains, and that it was manslaughter to go with women. It was foolishness to try to teach the Indians religion with anything but a rifle.

After a week's rest the caravan started on the march. They were now following the Sweetwater River upstream. The going became rugged as they passed through its wild canyons toward the great Continental Divide.

THE STAMPEDE

The caravan stretched out in single file for two miles across the plain in the shimmering midday heat. Riding at the head of the column, Fitzpatrick and the pilot squinted at the hazy horizon. They had expected to reach Independence Rock that day. Here prairie travelers rested and scrawled their names on the great rock that made a solitary landmark on the level plain.

The missionary party, with Marcus's wagon and their cattle, marched through the clouds of alkali dust at the end of the column. Sister Eliza sat among the baggage in the springless wagon in pious endurance. Narcissa, who was driving, licked her parched lips and clucked to the lagging horses.

At the head of the column a scout rode up to Fitz-patrick. "There's buffalo ahead. Plenty. They are coming this way. Looks like a stampede," he said.

Soon the travelers could see the black herds pouring out of the low hills ahead. The avalanche came rushing on, at right angles to the column. The caravan was in immediate danger of being trampled under the hoofs of the thunder-ing herd. Horses and mules were rearing with fright. "Close up! Close up!" The order was shouted down the line. The hunters raced ahead, firing at the leaders of the oncoming herds. But the maddened buffalo still charged directly on. It seemed that nothing could save the caravan from annihilation.

At the last moment the hunters, firing and shouting, managed to turn the leading bulls, and the great array swerved in a long arc and galloped along parallel to the caravan until the vast herds had passed, raising dense clouds of dust and shaking the earth with the impact of the frantic charge.

The caravan had escaped one of the sudden perils that sometimes came so unexpectedly upon the travelers of these vast wastes.

SOUTH PASS, JULY 4, 1836

For hours the marchers filed through the sagebrush desert. There was little to suggest that they were in the great South

Pass, the gateway to the Oregon country. At the camp at Pacific Springs they looked on the first water they had seen that flowed toward the sunset. In the lift of their spirits it seemed that they had almost reached their goal.

What was more certain was that they were nearing the rendezvous in the Green River Valley, which lay just ahead.

The order to halt and close up came down the line. Fitzpatrick, on a slight rise, was gazing through his glass at swift-moving specks far ahead. Were they elk, hostile Indians, or mountain men? He was soon able to make out horsemen at full gallop. A white flag waved from a gun barrel—a peace sign. He could see flashes of rifle fire and puffs of white smoke now. They could hear yells, howls, and the bark of the Indian warcry.

The wild riders came roaring down the line in full charge, hanging under the necks of their lathering ponies. It was a welcoming party from the rendezvous, celebrating the Fourth of July in mountain style.

Now the caravan began whooping and firing in reply. The Spaldings retired to the wagon, but Narcissa sat her horse, erect beside Marcus, her face glowing with excitement at the barbaric onrush, her pulses quickening to its splendid violence.

The welcoming party pulled up, leaped from their horses, and crowded around the awesome sight—the first white women to come through the South Pass.

THE RENDEZVOUS IN GREEN RIVER VALLEY
HORSE CREEK, WYOMING, JULY 1836

Narcissa had never seen so many Indians. There were two thousand of them camped along the level valley floor from which abruptly rose towering ranges and jagged mountain peaks. Wild cavalcades of Snakes and Flatheads galloped by, painted, feathered, and befurred in savage splendor. The Nez Percés too were there, eagerly awaiting the missionaries.

A procession of Indian women in beautiful white doeskin dresses rode out to meet them. They saluted their two white sisters with kisses, as they had been told was the custom. Eliza got out her Bible at once and went to work, reading to a circle of eager squaws who could not understand a word she was saying.

Narcissa thought the mountain men—there were some four hundred of them—were as savage as the Indians but much more interesting. The mission tent was a center of attraction for curious trappers, who hung around for a glimpse of the only white women many of them had seen in years. Narcissa gave them smiles and tea and listened to mountain talk and lore of the Rockies.

These were the wild and shaggy mountain men in their greasy fringed buckskins from which dangled the scalps of their enemies. Their bearded and weatherbeaten faces were framed in long hair that hung to their shoulders. What would the girls at Miss Willard's Seminary think if they could see her now in this strange company?

There were Jim Bridger, the famous trail scout, and Kit

Carson, a small man with a gentle face, who could "lick his weight in wildcats." "He's the gamecock of the wilderness, and he knows the mountains blindfolded from here to Santa Fe and California," the trappers told her. Joe Meek confided to her that he himself was a Methodist and read the Bible when he could get one. She listened to Black Harris, with his powder-marked face, tell tall tales of the mountains in a jargon that was stranger than the Missouri dialect that she had thought so amusing. One of Black Harris's yarns was taken down by George Ruxton, who heard him tell it to a lady. The conversation ran like this:

"Well, Mr. Harris, I hear you're a great traveler."

"Traveler, marm—this niggur's no traveler; I ar' a trapper, marm, a mountain man, wagh!"

"Well, Mr. Harris, trappers are great travelers, and you goes over a sight of ground in your pershinations, I'll be bound to say."

"A sight, marm, this coon's gone over, if that's the way your stick floats. I've trapped beaver on the Platte and Arkansas, and way up on Missouri and Yallerstone; I've trapped on Columbia, on Lewis Fork, and Green River; I've trapped, marm, on Grand River and Heely Gila. I've fought the Black Foot (and bad Injuns they are); I've raised the hair of more than one Apache, an' made a Rapaho 'come' afore now; I've trapped in heav'n, in airth, and hell, and, scalp my old head, marm, but I've seen a putrefied forest."

The story went on. The trappers in the dead of winter had come upon a prairie where the grass was green with summer and the birds sang in the trees. When Harris shot one its head went spinning off, still singing, and he found that its body was made of stone. So were the grass and trees.

"Young Sublette comes up, and he'd been clerking down to

the fort on Platte so he know'd something. He looks and looks, and scrapes the tree with his butcher knife, and snaps the grass like pipe stems, and breaks the leaves a-snappin' like Californy shells.

" 'What's all this, boy?' I asks.

" 'Putrefactions,' says he, looking smart, 'putrefactions, or I'm a niggur.' "

"La, Mr. Harris," says the lady. "Putrefactions, why, did the leaves and the trees, and the grass, smell bad?"

"Smell bad, marm," says Black Harris. "Would a skunk stink if he wuz froze to stone?" *

At this the trappers who stood solemnly listening and knew the story by heart exploded in roars of laughter.

These were the men who knew the trails and wild valleys and mountain passes of an immense wasteland. They had learned its vast expanses like a book and were masters of the curious arts and crafts by which white and red men survived its burning summers and blizzard-swept winters. Soon they were to guide the white-topped trains that would sweep across the continent in the march of American destiny to the Pacific.

As they crowded about this beautiful woman their eyes shone with wistful memories of a world they had long ago deserted and would never know again. It was a world that she too had left behind, for different reasons, but would never forget in the long and lonely vigils among the savage people of the wilderness to whom she was now dedicated.

Except for their smelling rather strongly of beaver bait, Narcissa found these strange men fascinating. The savage

* George Frederick Ruxton, *Life in the Far West*. Norman, Oklahoma: University of Oklahoma Press, 1951.

mountain men and the civilized woman sensed a strange tie that bound both forever to the West.

White traders plied the red men with watered-down alcohol and relieved them of their furs and all movable property. Trappers, in the ecstasy of their annual drunk, gambled away horses, Indian wives, and shirts. The company agents gathered in the fur bales of the trappers in exchange for ammunition and supplies.

When the last fur pack had been bartered and the last cup of firewater had been gulped, the high festival of the mountains came to an end. The circus was over. The annual orgy of the Wild West was finished. Shaky Indians with dreary hangovers drifted off to the wilderness to scalp and rob their enemies; mountain men returned to their traps in the icy streams of Cache Valley or Absoraka to peel off the hides of the vanishing beaver. With Fitzpatrick at its head, the company caravan filed briskly eastward over the pass, a fortune in furs on its pack mules.

Marcus said farewell to the mountain men. He came to Fitzpatrick to ask what the charges were for his protection and guidance across the prairie. The partisan replied, "And what, may I ask, do you charge me for *your* services as doctor on the expedition?"

Whitman made an impatient gesture. "Why, nothing at all, of course."

"Then I shall charge you the same," replied Fitzpatrick. Brave men who had shared weeks together on the trail did not owe each other in terms that money could measure. These two great pioneers shook hands, said, "Adios," and parted to the East and to the West.

The excitement and exuberance of the rendezvous was

saddened for the mission by a deep disappointment. The Reverend Samuel Parker had not arrived. An Indian messenger brought his letter. It told how he had intended to come with the Walla Walla Indians, but when he found that they were not going to follow the regular trail but take a wandering course, hunting as they went, through the grim mountains of the Divide, he had changed his plans. He had gone down the Columbia to Fort Vancouver and planned to return to the States by ship. He recommended the Grande Ronde and the valley of the Clearwater as good sites for their missions among the Nez Percés. Whitman had counted on Parker to guide and counsel them through the trackless wastes beyond the mountains, to the Columbia.

While Marcus was pondering this gloomy predicament a stranger walked into the mission camp. There was no mistaking his Yankee twang.

This man was Nathaniel Wyeth, the enterprising New Englander who had ventured and just lost a fortune in the wilderness. He was a promoter of free enterprise who had started west half a century too soon. He told them about the Hudson's Bay Company's prosperous establishment at Fort Vancouver on the Columbia, and of the fertile Willamette valley where Jason and Daniel Lee had planted their now prospering Methodist mission in 1834.

Best of all, Wyeth introduced Marcus to two British fur traders, partisans of the Hudson's Bay Company, who were starting on their return to the Oregon country. Their names were Thomas McKay and John McLeod. This was the first time the British had rendezvoused with American fur traders. It was among the duties of these two gentlemen to discourage American fur companies from entering the Oregon country, which the Hudson's Bay Company regarded as strictly British territory. However, American missionaries wanting to Christianize the Indians were another matter. The British traders agreed to help the mission party along the rough trail to the Columbia. Though he did not know it, Mr. McLeod was taking the first step toward losing Oregon for his country. If Whitman insisted on taking his ridiculous wagon along, it was his back that would be broken, not the Englishmen's. To attempt to take women through the mountains was, in their private opinion, little short of murder. If, however, the experiment were to succeed it would be interesting. These Britishers were men of good breeding and decency.

The missionaries were grateful to have the protection and guidance of these experienced trappers through the wild country that lay ahead. Their first stretch would be to Fort Hall on the Snake River.

DOWN THE SNAKE

The Snake made its winding way westward out of the Rockies in a great S to join the Columbia nearly a thousand miles away, crossing a volcanic land of black basalt that had once been a sea bottom. Through eons of time the Snake had carved deep canyons as it wound and twisted through some of the wildest country on the continent. It was the Snake that had broken the heart of Wilson Price Hunt and the starving Astorians as they staggered toward the Pacific twenty-five years before. It was toward the

Snake that the Hudson's Bay Company brigade and the missionaries now made their way from the Green River Valley.

Mr. McLeod turned in his saddle and looked back down the column as it fell into line. He waved his hat, touched his horse's side with his heel, and shouted, "Forward." The drivers yelled to their mules, and the long line was set in motion. Behind the leader rode the Spaldings and the Whitmans. Pack mules and horses followed in single file. Marcus's wagon and the Indian boys with their cattle brought up the rear. Alongside them Snake and Flathead squaws rode with their papooses swung from the saddle bows, shrilly scolding their ponies and dogs. Indian braves dashed up and down the line in a disorderly array, emitting blood-curdling yells in the excitement of getting under way.

The brigade made its way across the Green River to Hams Fork, where it turned northward to the Bear River and followed this stream as the sun set behind the purple wall of the Wasatch Mountains. The Soda Springs country was rough and steep, and the women clung to the horses, which stepped cautiously along narrow trails and climbed perilously up mountain walls.

On July 25, Narcissa wrote:

Husband has had a tedious time with the wagon today. It got stuck in the creek this morning when crossing, and he was obliged to wade considerably in getting it out. After that, in going between the mountains, on the side of one, so steep that it was difficult for horses to pass, the wagon was upset twice; did not wonder at this at all; it was a great wonder that it was not turning somersaults continually. It was not very grateful to my feelings to see him wearing out with such excessive fatigue, as I am obliged to.

Once set, Marcus was not a man to give up.

There was no longer any fresh meat, and even Narcissa gagged on the unvarying fare of dried buffalo meat without bread.

(. . . if you knew how well I should relish even the dryest morsel, you would save every piece carefully.) Do not think I regret coming. No, far from it! I would not go back for a world. I am contented and happy, notwithstanding I sometimes get very hungry and weary. Have six weeks' steady journey before us. Feel sometimes as if it were a long time to be traveling. Long for rest, but must not murmur.

So far the cattle were holding up quite well, and there was milk for tea and coffee and trail-made butter. As they advanced, McLeod sent small bands of trappers into the mountains to take beaver. The Indians stayed with the brigade for protection. They were going through the country of their enemies, the dreaded Blackfeet.

THE RELUCTANT WAGON

Marcus wrastled the wagon over the mountains, trying to keep pace with the brigade. At night he dreamed that he was pushing wagon trains up precipices toward the sky. Just as he reached the top they would tumble back upon him, and all would plunge into the rushing torrents below. He opened his eyes to feel Narcissa shaking him out of the nightmare. Narcissa really wished the wagon at the bottom of the river.

On July 28 she wrote:

One of the axle-trees of the wagon broke today; was a little rejoiced, for we were in hopes they would leave it, and have no more trouble with it. Our rejoicing was in vain for they are making a cart of the back wheels, this afternoon, and lashing the fore wheels to it—intending to make it through in some shape or other. They are so resolute and untiring in their efforts they will probably succeed.

Had some fresh fish for breakfast and some antelope for supper, sent us by Mr. McLeod and other friends in camp. Thus the Lord provides, and smoothes all our ways for us, giving us strength.

"Look, the fort! The fort!" The shout went down the line. From the ridge they could see the log palisade of Fort Hall and the rushing waters of the great Snake. "Fort Hall was built by Captain Wyeth, a gentleman from Boston, whom we saw at Rendezvous on his way east," wrote Narcissa. Wyeth had just sold it to the British.

Captain Thing of the Hudson's Bay Company was the present commander. He welcomed the mission with British heartiness. After a good dinner graced with the luxury of mountain bread—coarse flour and water mixed with buffalo grease—Captain Thing proudly showed them his garden. There were turnips, peas, and onions, and there was a cornpatch—all very seedy and discouraged, but it was a pioneer garden, the first in all that wild land, and it held promises for the future.

On August 4 the brigade started down the south bank of the Snake. "The Indians all leave us today except one or two, who go with us to assist in driving the cattle—

Kentuck, who went with Mr. Parker last year, and the chief Rottenbelly." The departing Indians pleaded with the mission to go with them, but Whitman knew the brigade was safer and swifter and so firmly refused.

Perilously they crossed rushing streams that tumbled into the canyons of the Snake. Clouds of mosquitoes tortured man and beast. The heat was terrific. Two of the pack horses went over the falls; it took an hour to recover the badly bruised animals. As the fatigue and physical strain grew almost unbearable, valiant Narcissa prayed her prayers of faith and counted her blessings. At each night's camp a great peace came upon her spirit. "Surely the children of Israel could not have been more sensible of the pillar of fire by night than we have been of that hand that has led us thus safely on."

The Spaldings were both ill, and tempers flared under the terrible physical strains.

THE LITTLE TRUNK

On Friday, August 12, there was fresh fish. The great silver salmon were coming up the rivers, and the Indians at the salmon fishery were taking them with nets and spears.

Narcissa wrote to her sister:

Friday Eve. Aug. 12th. Dear Harriet, the little trunk you gave me has come with me so far, and now I must leave it here alone. Poor little trunk, I am sorry to leave thee; thou must abide here alone, and no more by thy presence remind me of my dear Harriet. Twenty miles below the falls on Snake River this shall be thy place of rest. Farewell, little trunk, I thank thee for thy faithful services, and I have been cheered by thy presence so long. Thus we scatter as we go along.

The trunk had come a long way and had been wet in many fordings. At the very beginning it had gone overboard into the river on that first gay sleigh ride from Elmira, New York, to Williamsport, after the wedding.

13th—Saturday. Dear Harriet, Mr. McKay has asked the privilege of taking the little trunk along, so that my soliloquy about it last night was for naught.

The custom of the country is to possess nothing and then you will lose nothing while traveling.

GLENN'S FERRY

They crossed the Snake River to the north bank.

The river is divided by two islands into three branches, and is fordable. The packs are placed upon the tops of the highest horses and in this way we crossed without wetting. Two of the tallest horses were selected to carry Mrs. Spalding and myself over. Mr. McLeod gave me his and rode mine. The last branch we rode as much as half a mile in crossing and against the current, too, which made it hard for the horses, the water being up to their sides. Husband had considerable difficulty in crossing the cart. Both cart and mules were turned upside down in the river and entangled in the harness. The mules would have been drowned but for a desperate struggle to get them ashore. Then after putting two of the strongest horses before the cart, and two men swimming behind to steady it, they succeeded in getting it across. I once thought that crossing streams would be the most dreaded part of the journey. I can now cross the most difficult stream without the least fear.

One of Narcissa's biographers, examining this particular ford long afterward, wrote, "Few men could be found today who would undertake to make this ford under any condition short of life itself." *

Narcissa and Eliza crossed plenty of other rivers. Each had its special hazards, but the women took them all in their stride with a cool and unfailing courage.

SNAKE FORT

After the crossing to the north shore at Glenn's Ferry, the fur brigade left the Snake, making a direct march to the Boise River. This route was like a bowstring across the long bend of the Snake and saved two days over the south shore route. McLeod with the strongest animals went ahead, leaving the mission to follow. They came upon the hot springs, where Narcissa boiled a bit of dried salmon in five minutes. She relished the sweet mealy hawthorn berries which she picked by the streams where they camped.

At noon on August 17 they rode into Snake Fort (Fort Boise). This was Mr. McKay's pride, for he himself had supervised the building of it two years before. A hearty dinner awaited the party, and that evening Narcissa put her washing to soak overnight. "This morning I finished washing before breakfast. This is the third time I have washed since I have left home—once at Fort Williams and once at Rendezvous."

* Miles Cannon. *Waiilatpu, Its Rise and Fall, 1836–1847*. Boise, Idaho: Capital News Job Rooms, 1915.

Five of the exhausted cattle were left at the fort. Marcus argued doggedly to the last for the wagon. He must take the first wagon to the Columbia. Everyone was violently against him. Some refused to go on if they had to take that terrible wagon. Gray even promised he would come back for it—he never did—and Marcus finally gave in and sadly left the wagon behind.

In spite of their objection to Sunday travel, the mission had to overtake McLeod's party. Leaving Snake Fort on Sunday afternoon, August 21, they recrossed the Snake near where the Boise River empties into it. This time the crossing was quite a lark. The river was too deep to ford. "We easily found a canoe, made of rushes and willows, on which we placed ourselves and our saddles (Sister Spalding and myself), when two Indians on horseback, each with a rope attached to the canoe, towed us over. O! If father and mother and the girls could have seen us in our snug little canoe, floating on the water," wrote the buoyant Narcissa.

The Whitmans rode ahead to overtake McLeod. The Spaldings followed more slowly with the worn-out cattle and horses. The advance party camped at the "Lone Tree," a landmark on the trail near the Powder River, and left their tent for the Spaldings, who would need it on their slower journey. On the morning of August 28 the Whitmans rode out on a hilltop and saw before them the fabled Grande Ronde valley. "It is a circular plain, surrounded by lofty mountains, and has a beautiful stream coursing through it, skirted with quite large timber." This was the valley where the Indian tribes came to dig their winter supply of the curious camass root. "It resembles an onion in shape and color; when cooked is very sweet and tastes like a fig."

That afternoon they ascended the pine-covered slopes of the Blue Mountains. After the hot plains they reveled in the scented gloom of the forests, even though they had to struggle desperately through tangles of fallen timber. Along the forest path were singing birds and familiar flowers that reminded them of home. Next morning Narcissa woke wonderfully rested. A surge of magnificent health and strength went through her as she mounted her horse and the party began the last descent of the Blue Mountains. As the slope became precipitous the horses' tender unshod feet slipped on the black basaltic rock. They zigzagged down the perpendicular cliffs of the awful chasm. The travelers had seen plenty of the roughest mountain riding in America on their journey, but this descent of the Blue Mountains was the most terrifying.

The party now ascended a long ridge and rode along its summit till sunset, looking for water and a campsite. In the far distance they could see the cone-shaped peaks of two snow-capped mountains, Mount Hood and Mount Helena, against a sunset of dusty rose and acid green. Like Moses on Pisgah, the pilgrims beheld at last the promised land. They stood silent, drinking in the majestic vision. That night Narcissa's heart overflowed as she wrote, "Dearest Mother, let me tell you how I am sustained of the Lord in all this journey."

On August 30 they rested, grazed their exhausted animals, and sent back for two packhorses that had given out on the trail. Narcissa gathered ripe cherries, which were growing in abundance. Mr. McLeod, as was customary, prepared to ride on to Walla Walla to announce the arrival of the party. He told Narcissa about the delicious Walla Walla muskmelons and promised to bring her a large one.

Next day was a long hard pull through sand with no water. Marcus's Indian horse was a hard rider "in every gait except a gallop. . . . So for the last six days we have galloped most of the way where the ground would admit of it." That night they camped within eight miles of Fort Walla Walla on the Columbia.

THE ROOSTER CROWS

This was September 1. It was to be a great day, the end at last of the long trek. Everyone was up at dawn and dressed for the occasion in whatever civilized clothes had survived. Narcissa primped and tied a ribbon on her bonnet. The doctor wore a necktie, a white shirt, and his black tailcoat. They snatched a cup of coffee and were off. The horses caught the excitement and broke into a gallop. The gay cavalcade raced by the gardens within two miles of the fort and broke into wild cheers as the great river, the Columbia, came in sight. There, under the terraced river bluffs, was Fort Walla Walla!

Three horsemen rode out from the fort, waving their hats. One was Mr. McLeod, who introduced them to his friends, Mr. Pambrun, the factor, and Mr. Townsend, the traveling naturalist. At the fort they were just having breakfast. With a long sigh Narcissa sank into a cushioned armchair beside Mr. Pambrun. At the breakfast table she demolished enormous helpings of fresh salmon, potatoes, tea, and heavenly bread and butter and slices of juicy melon. "You cannot imagine what an appetite these rides in the mountains give a person," she said to the beaming Mr. Pambrun as she attacked another slice of bread and butter. "I wish some of the feeble ones in the States could have a ride over the mountains," she added between mouthfuls. "They would say like me, victuals, even the plainest kind, never relished so well before."

Just then a rooster that had wandered in through the open door crowed magnificently. Narcissa rose and curtsied.

"Ah, madam, he is giving you a French welcome to the Columbia," exclaimed the delighted Mr. Pambrun. The whole party burst into a roar of laughter and applause.

Mr. Pambrun had provided for the Whitmans a room with bunks in one of the bastions of the fort. Its walls bristled with rifles, and behind the door was a loaded brass cannon. Mr. Pambrun said it was a great persuader when he had to argue with the Indians.

After breakfast he proudly showed them the novelties of the place. The dooryard was filled with hens, turkeys, and pigeons. "In another place we saw cows and goats in abundance, and I think the largest and fattest cattle and swine I ever saw," wrote Narcissa.

Three days later the Spaldings rode into the compound with the jaded cattle. Mr. Pambrun welcomed the travelers with another celebration, and the tables again groaned with all the bounty of a Columbia welcome.

So they had come to the goal at long last. It was hard to believe that Narcissa had been the prim spinster of Angelica less than a year ago. What a year it had been—

the sudden marriage, Pittsburgh, Cincinnati, St. Louis, Liberty, and the strange adventurous prairie honeymoon. Through the hardships and hazards she had been exquisitely happy, no matter what the end might be. Plainsmen, mountain men, red men—she had ridden with them all in a wild splendid wayfaring across America, the first of all the valiant women who would follow the heartbreak trail to Oregon.

Riding by her side was the best husband in the whole world, she thought; her friend, protector, and wise counselor. Always she had worn the sword and shield of her faith in God, and she had a talent for happiness that shone brightest when the going was toughest. These she would need in the long days of physical labor and personal danger that lay ahead.

PART TWO
THE HEART OF DARKNESS
Waiilatpu

THE OLD TRAILS

Old wheel ruts deep still mark the trace
Where the prairie schooners passed this place—
A name faint marked on a crumbling stone;
In the desert dust a whitened bone.
Bleached bone in the prairie dust
And iron wheel rim turned to rust,
The shapes forgotten, but still we find
The living image of the mind.
In cloud forms in the wind-swept sky
The long processions still roll by,
And drifting high above the peak,
Across the blue the white-tops streak.
The dream and the image long shall be
Bright in American memory.

Down the Columbia
September 6–12, 1836

"I feel remarkably well and rested, do not need to lounge at all, and so it is with us all," wrote Narcissa during her first week at Walla Walla. "Messrs. McLeod and Townsend left for Vancouver today, but Mr. McLeod is so loaded as not to be able to give us a comfortable passage."

To start the missions it was necessary first of all to have tools and supplies. These could be had only from Fort Vancouver three hundred miles down the Columbia. Whitman and Spalding found it necessary to make this trip, and their wives were determined to go with them.

Mr. Pambrun is going by himself next week and offers us a passage with him. Mr. Pambrun is from Canada, and much of the gentleman in his appearance.

If we were obliged to go on horseback, I think I should not wish to undertake it, but we are going in a boat and it will not take us more than six days to go there. A very agreeable change and I think I shall enjoy it as well as to stay here.

The boats were two hollowed logs some thirty feet long. Narcissa sat amidships among the carefully stowed baggage. Her eyes sparkled with excitement as the canoes shot down the smooth current under the skilled strokes of the Indian paddlers. This was another thrilling experience in her discovery of America.

There were places where the river tumbled over rocky falls and rushed through terrifying gorges—the Chute, the Dalles, and the Cascades. Here they went through the ritual of the portage. The Indians shouldered the baggage and the canoes and carried them overland around the falls, while the passengers followed on foot.

As she waited at the first portage while Marcus explored, Narcissa felt something queer. Reaching her hand to the back of her neck, she discovered—fleas! Looking down at her dress, she saw that it was covered with swarming armies of them. She was speechless, frantic, more terrified than if there had been an Indian attack. She rushed after Marcus. Together they brushed the advancing armies from the pleats and folds of Narcissa's dress. For the time being she was saved, but before they had passed the Dalles everyone in the party was itching and squirming.

They made their last camp at the sawmill within five miles of the fort and sent an Indian squaw ahead to announce their arrival. Next morning everyone dressed up for the occasion. As the canoes rounded the point, there before them lay the great fort with its flags flying, and in the harbor two British ships in gala rig. At the landing stood a group of gentlemen. As the two women stepped from the canoe, a tall white-haired man came forward and offered Narcissa his arm. It was the great factor of Vancouver himself, Dr. John McLoughlin.

After the introductions and greetings Narcissa asked, "Why are all the flags flying? Is it a holiday?"

"Ah, madame, it is a day of celebration unique in our history. We are honoring the first white women ever to descend the Columbia," replied the factor with a gallant bow.

FORT VANCOUVER INTERLUDE

Vancouver was a world unbelievable to the pilgrims fresh from the thousands of miles of wilderness. It was a fairy tale, fantastic, incredible. Here, at the end of the long trail, was civilization again—houses, gardens, schools, people with fine manners and clothes, and British order and hospitality.

Here was the center and citadel of the British fur trade of the Northwest, and here British ships arrived from London with cargoes and supplies for the remote forts and trading stations of the valley of the Columbia. Along the noble river three thousand acres of cultivated land tilled by a hundred Indians provided food for the seven hundred inhabitants of the station. A forest of magnificent pine, cedar, and fir extended for thirty-five miles eastward to where the snow-crowned peaks of the Presidential Range rose against the sky.

For days the two women viewed and admired the novelties and wonders of the place. The fort itself was a palisaded enclosure two hundred and fifty by one hundred and fifty yards. Within this were thirty-five buildings. These included officers' quarters, storehouses, workshops, a hospital, and a school where the fifty halfbreed children of the fort learned English and the three Rs. A sawmill, gristmill, and threshing machine turned and ground out food and lumber. Blacksmiths, wheelwrights, carpenters, coopers, masters of a dozen skills and crafts, busily plied their trades.

The visitors promenaded with delight through the neat gardens, vineyards, and orchards. Here were apples, peaches, plums, pears, figs, and grapes, bearing abundantly out of the rich Oregon soil. The gardens were green with an unending variety of vegetables, and the walks were lined with strawberry beds. Herds of sheep, cattle, and swine provided a variety of meats, and the tables groaned with varied foods and delicacies. After the feasts there were always wines and cigars and good talk. French was spoken more than English, and many of the men knew several of the Indian tongues. According to legend, the orchards and vineyards had sprung from seed which a gentleman had pocketed at a great dinner in London and brought to Oregon.

The Hudson's Bay Company was not in business to encourage American settlements in Oregon territory, but

McLoughlin agreed that missions to the Indians would be a good thing. He offered to sell supplies and tools and furnish cattle to the Americans until they could get started, which he said would take two years. For a number of good reasons Whitman and Spalding decided to start separate missions. But they would go up the Columbia together and select their locations, while their wives awaited their return at Vancouver.

It was a busy time for Narcissa. She tutored the factor's intelligent daughter Maria. "I sing about an hour every evening with the children, teaching them new tunes, at the request of Dr. McLoughlin. Thus I am wholly occupied, and can scarcely find as much time as I want to write."

There were weekly afternoon rides with Mrs. McLoughlin. "She keeps her old habit of riding gentleman fashion. This is the universal custom of the Indian women, and they have saddles with high backs and fronts. We have been recommended to use these saddles, as a more easy way of riding, but we have never seen the necessity of changing our fashion."

Dr. McLoughlin urged the two women to stay at the fort for the winter while their husbands built the missions. Narcissa would be having a baby in the early spring, and the doctor argued that it would be easier for her at the fort than in the wilderness. But the women were anxious to begin the work for which they had traveled so hazardously and far. On October 18 Spalding arrived. He had come down the river with the Montreal Express, which brought the mail across the continent twice a year. He and Whitman had selected their locations. Whitman was building a cabin among the Cayuse Indians, about twenty-five miles from Walla Walla. Spalding had chosen to go to the Nez Percés, about one hundred miles in the interior, at Lapwai on the Clearwater River.

Oct. 18. The Montreal Express came this afternoon, and a general time of rejoicing it is to everyone. News of distant friends, both sad and pleasing.

Mr. Spalding has come with it and brought a letter from my husband, filled with pleasing information. The Lord has been with them since they left us, and has prospered them beyond all expectations. They have each selected a location. My husband remains there to build, while Mr. Spalding comes after us. Cheering thought this, to be able to make a beginning in our pleasing work so soon.

The Nez Percés had shaken their heads when they learned that the Whitmans were going to establish their mission with the Cayuses. Narcissa remembered the Nez Percés' warning. "They do not like to have us stop with the Cayouses. Say they (Nez Percés) do not have difficulty with the white men, as the Cayouses do and that we shall find it so."

"IT IS INDEED A LOVELY SITUATION"
WAIILATPU, DECEMBER 1836

The new home at Waiilatpu was not finished when Narcissa arrived at Fort Walla Walla. Marcus, Mr. Gray, and the two hired Owyhees worked for three weeks before it was ready. While Narcissa waited as the guest of the hospitable Pambruns she taught Mr. Pambrun's Indian wife how to speak English.

Dec. 8. Received intelligence that husband was coming to-morrow to remove our effects and myself to our new home. It is an agreeable thought to be so near a fixed location after journeying so long.

We arrived here on the tenth, distance twenty-five miles from Walla Walla. Found a house reared and the lean-to enclosed, a good chimney and fireplace, and the floor laid. No windows or door except blankets. My heart truly leaped for joy as I alighted from my horse, entered and seated myself before a pleasant fire (for it was now night). It occurred to me that my dear parents had made a similar beginning, and perhaps a more difficult one than ours. We had neither straw, bedstead, nor table, nor anything to make them of except green cottonwood.

They sat on the blankets, looking into the fire.

"To think that it has not been a year since we were married," said Narcissa. "We hardly knew each other before then."

"And what a year it has been! So much has happened. It seems as though we had lived several lifetimes together," said Marcus thoughtfully. "Tomorrow we will start a new life—from the very beginning, with nothing but our own hands, our faith, and God's help."

Next morning Narcissa stood in the doorway and looked out for the first time at the new world where they were to live, to struggle, and to conquer.

It is, indeed, a lovely situation. We are on a beautiful level, a peninsula formed by the branches of the Walla Walla River, upon the base of which our house stands, on the southeast corner, near the shore of the main river. To run a fence across to the opposite river, on the north from our house—this, with the river, would enclose 300 acres of good land for cultivation, all directly under the eye. . . . This is all the woodland we can see; beyond them, as far as the eye can reach, plains and mountains appear. On the east, a few rods from the house, is a range of small hills, covered with bunchgrass, a very excellent food for animals, and upon which they subsist during the winter, even digging it from under the snow.

This was Waiilatpu—the place of rye grass.

THE CAYUSES. THE FIRST YEAR, 1837

There were not many Indians at the mission during the first winter. They had gone to the Grande Ronde to hunt and dig camass roots. In the spring the tribe returned to their camping ground on the Walla Walla about three miles from the mission.

They came to the mission in droves at all times of the day. The squaws crowded the kitchen, bringing fleas and dirt. The Indian children pried everywhere until patient Narcissa grew frantic. She finally made a rule that Indians were to be admitted to only one room—"the Indian room," as she called it. The Indians complained about this and resented it.

The Whitmans held Sunday services for the Indians, and these services were well attended. They found that the Indians would have to be taught in the Nez Percé tongue—Christianity and the Bible would have to be filtered through the Nez Percé language. How much of the translated doctrine the Indians understood was a question.

But there were encouraging things too. The Cayuses did

not steal. There was no raw alcohol; the Hudson's Bay Company had seen to that. Narcissa was grateful that the Cayuses wore clothes, for her Puritan eyes abhorred nudity. Best of all, the Indians really wanted to learn.

When Narcissa started children's classes the Cayuse youngsters came daily. They loved to sing and eagerly learned hymns that had been translated into Nez Percé. In time she contrived to write out a fifty-two-page book of Nez Percé words in the English alphabet. A class of intelligent pupils delighted in wrestling with this new sign language on a blackboard placed on the shady side of the cabin wall.

The Cayuse chiefs, old Umtippe and young Tilaukaik, and their braves, considered labor unmanly. They never worked themselves but enjoyed watching the doctor, Gray, and the two Owyhees sawing, hammering, hoeing, and building cabins and the gristmill. The new T-shaped mission building was slowly rising, and the fields yielded fine crops.

SPRING SONG, 1837

Whitman squatted on his haunches, farmer fashion.

He scooped up a handful of the black soil and ran it lovingly through his fingers. Spring was in the air, and he was eager to break the virgin soil into long furrows for planting; eager to see the plowshare shearing the loamy soil and to smell the clean smell of newly turned earth. In his dream he could see the green blades springing up and filling the whole land of Oregon with a golden harvest of wheat and corn in the years to come. New life was at hand. Soon there would be a cradle song. Their child would be the first white American born in Oregon.

It was on March 14, Narcissa's twenty-ninth birthday, that the baby came, with Marcus Whitman and Mrs. Pambrun helping. Narcissa pulled through with flying colors, as she always did in a crisis. The baby was a fine girl, and they called her Alice Clarissa after her two grandmothers. "She is the loveliest birthday present anyone ever had," said Narcissa, smiling, as Marcus leaned over the bed and kissed her.

The March wind rustled the rye grass, the neat rows of green spears thrust up, and Narcissa's lullaby drifted to the river, which was rushing full in the gray spring rain.

The arrival of a white baby at the Whitmans' cabin was the big news in the Walla Walla country. It seemed that everybody for miles around dropped in to see. Besides starting the spring plowing, Marcus washed diapers and did the cooking till Narcissa could get organized. "An affectionate husband, who, as a physician and nurse, exceeds all I ever knew," commented Narcissa, writing home to tell about the new baby.

Her complexion, her size, and dress, etc., all excite a deal of wonder; for they never raise a child here except they are lashed tight to a board, and the girls' heads undergo the flattening process. I have not yet described my babe to you. I think her grandmother would willingly own her as one of her number of babies, could she see her. Her hair is a light brown, and we think will be like her aunts Jane and Harriet. She is plump and large, holds her head up finely, and looks about considerably. She weighs ten pounds. Fee-low-Ki-Kei a kind, friendly Indian, called to see her the next day after she was born. Said she was

Cayouse te-mi (Cayouse girl), because she was born on Cayouse wai-tis (Cayouse land). He told us her arrival was expected by all the people of the country—the Nez Percés, Cayouses and Walla Wallapoos Indians, and, now she has arrived,
it would soon be heard of by them all, and we must write to
our land and tell our parents and friends of it. The whole tribe
are highly pleased because we allow her to be called a Cayouse
girl.

But I *must* close. I cannot say how much we need your
prayers, and must beg of you again and again to pray unceas-
ingly for us. If you would have us live, and not die, you must
pray.

It had not always been easy for even the best Christians
back in New York State to teach the Ten Commandments
or even obey them. But Narcissa knew that this was where
she must begin if ever she was to teach Christianity to the
black-eyed Cayuse children who came every day, willing
and eager to learn, when the tribe was in its neighboring
camp. She must get the ideas across in the Nez Percé
tongue, of which she was almost as ignorant as the children
were of English. The lessons became a two-way exchange
in which they all learned together. The hymns helped a lot.
She sang them beautifully, and the children soon learned
to join in and loved it. What they could sing together became easier to understand. The older Indians came to the
Sunday service which Marcus conducted regularly. Sometimes there were so many that the service had to be held
out of doors. It was an encouraging beginning to a long and
difficult task.

Besides the teaching there were the washing and baking
and cooking, which Narcissa managed to do over an open

fireplace while dreaming of a beautiful iron stove. After a visit from the Cayuses there was the cleaning up of mud and fleas. Through it all she kept her eye on lively little Alice and managed to keep her off the floor and, most of the time, in her lap. The child filled her heart with the most perfect happiness she had ever known.

Through the cabin window she could glimpse Marcus at the farm labor or talking with visiting Indians. There were times when her heart beat anxiously or froze with terror as she saw them make angry or threatening gestures. She fervently thanked God that Marcus always stood calm and firm until the terrible pantomime subsided. In the evening he told her of these disputes and of how he coped with the restless and uncertain moods of the Cayuses.

Narcissa became aware that at any time a flare-up of savage temper or some superstitious fear might bring down sudden and violent destruction upon the defenseless mission. The post was a little pool of light shining in the darkness of a Stone Age. They were on the edge of a volcano, and hidden fires were seething.

There was no human protection, there were no material defenses, only faith and prayer and God. For Marcus and Narcissa these were enough.

Our united choice would be to live and die here—to spend our lives for the salvation of this people. . . . We have ever been contented and happy, notwithstanding all our trials, and let come what will, we had rather die in the battle than to retreat, if the Lord will only appear for us and remove all that is in the way of His salvation; take up every stumbling block out of our hearts and from this mission, and prosper His own cause here. Our ardent prayer is, Lord let not this mission fail; for our Board says it is the last effort they shall make for the poor Indians.

The station was built on the old Chief Umtippe's land. Though he had no papers to prove it was his, he had given the Whitmans permission to use it. But occasionally the chief appeared and complained that he had received no recompense, that the whites were using Indian land and water and trees and air, but that the Indians had not been paid nor received presents. At times a racial anxiety, a prophetic premonition of a coming doom, swept through the Cayuse tepees and brought the chief to the mission.

When Parker first came he had told the Indians that they would be paid for their land. Jason Lee had accepted their horses but had given no gifts in return. The Indians considered this robbery. Whitman pointed out that the Indians had asked him to come and teach them, that he was there to do them good. If they wished him to go he would do so, but the tribe must decide this. The proposition was discussed and voted upon at the tribal councils, but always the majority wished the white teachers to remain.

THE TE-WAT

Richard, the Nez Percé boy, had long been a special favorite with Narcissa. He often brought in Indian gossip from the Cayuse village. One morning he remarked casually, "Ye-he-kis-kis has killed the bad Te-wat."

Narcissa straightened from the tub where she was bathing Alice. "How terrible! And why did he do it?"

"The Te-wat could not drive out the evil spirits, and so Ye-he-kis-kis' cousin died."

Narcissa's blood chilled with terror.

"The Te-wat went away without giving the family presents, so of course Ye-he-kis-kis killed the Te-wat. It is always done," Richard continued. "It is the custom of the ancient ones since the beginning of things."

Narcissa recalled with a shudder the terrible night when Marcus had watched by the side of Umtippe's sick wife. When it looked as if she were dying Umtippe had said to the doctor, "If she dies I will kill you." The squaw grew better, and Marcus retired from the case. Umtippe had then called in the great Te-wat (medicine man) from Walla Walla. There had been a wild night of chanting, drum-beating, and dancing. Next day the Te-wat said he had driven out the evil spirits. Umtippe gave him a horse and a blanket. After the Te-wat left, the squaw was again sick. Umtippe was furious and said the Te-wat should die.

The doctor had never refused a call from sick Indians. Fortunately all had recovered. He told the Cayuses that the Te-wats were bad men who deceived the Indians. Again Umtippe came to the doctor. He was very sick and wanted medicine. The doctor treated him. When it looked as if he would die, Narcissa was terrified. But the old chief pulled through.

Marcus told the Indians he would give them no gifts if his patients did not recover. Why should he pay them when he was trying to do them good? In his Sunday sermons he told them they must change their wicked ways and turn from superstition and murder. Such sinners were punished in hell. But the Cayuses said this was bad talk. He must speak only good words and tell them stories out of the

Bible. When the doctor refused to change his teaching to entertainment the Indians grew sulky and turned their cattle into the doctor's precious potato fields at night.

William Gray was an excellent carpenter, and he had helped both Whitman and Spalding build their stations. He had ambitions of his own to be both a doctor and a missionary. He wanted to be his own master. Without consulting Whitman, he started back to the States to get reinforcements and perhaps, while in the East, to study medicine. On the way he and his Flathead companions had a fight with the Sioux. There was a rumor among the mountain men, though it was never proved, that Gray saved his own life by sacrificing his Flathead companions to the Sioux. After attending lectures on medicine for sixteen weeks at Utica, New York, he assumed the title of doctor. But when he returned to the Columbia, Whitman curtly commented, "What can a man learn in sixteen weeks to entitle him to that distinction?"

A VISIT, NOVEMBER 1836

On a gray November day three Indians rode into the mission. They brought a message from Lapwai. Mrs. Spalding's baby was about to arrive, and would the doctor come at once. It was more than a hundred miles, across rough country, in bad weather, but Marcus never refused such calls. Narcissa pleaded that she and Alice Clarissa might come too. So they boarded up the mission windows and started off, Narcissa riding sidesaddle, with Alice in her arms. The rain turned to snow. The Indians pitched the leather lodge that Spalding had sent on the banks of the Walla Walla. In this shelter the Whitmans slept snug and dry through a night of wind and rain.

Next day they must ford the Snake River. Narcissa had done this more than once before, but this time, with Alice in her arms, she felt anxious. Her strong horse breasted the swift current bravely, however, and brought them safely through. The Spaldings welcomed them with open arms. When, two days later—November 15—the baby arrived, little Alice was wild with delight and wanted to hug her new friend all the time. The Reverend Mr. Spalding solemnly baptized both infants, to the great joy of their pious mothers. Because of snow, the Whitmans returned by way of the Snake, which raced through rocky canyons to the Columbia. Their Indian guide, who was greatly concerned for Alice, took them safely through the last wild rapid, and they came to Walla Walla. They found everything secure at the mission. It had been a great adventure for a baby not one year old.

The older Indians still solemnly attended the Sunday services Marcus held, and the young day scholars from the nearby lodges were learning to read under Narcissa's patient teaching. There was plenty of food for all that winter. Two Sandwich Islanders (Hawaiians) and two Indian boys were added to their helpers, and in the spring the Indians came from a distance to ask for seed. This delighted Whitman's farmer's heart, and he supplied them generously.

His crops had been abundant, and his cattle multiplied. The second winter had passed. The Whitmans counted their blessings and devoutly thanked God.

Marcus dreamed of what one hundred plows and six hundred hoes in Indian hands would bring forth. In his visions he saw the starving tribes nourished with fair gardens and farmyards abundant with cattle and fat hogs, and schools filled with eager dark-skinned students.

Infrequently travelers going to or coming from the States stopped at the mission. Jason Lee, who had crossed the mountains a year before the Whitmans, arrived from the Willamette and stayed a few days, regaling Marcus with large plans for his trip to the States, where he would spread the news of the wonders of Oregon and bring back abundant supplies to the Willamette Mission.

If Mr. Lee could obtain such support for the Methodist mission, Marcus decided that he could appeal to the Board for needed supplies to expand the mission work on the upper Columbia with equal success. He talked over his ideas and plans with Mr. Spalding. They agreed on a joint letter to the Board. Spalding would write it, and Marcus would list the itemized supplies they so desperately needed.

THE JOINT LETTER

Marcus sat at his desk, writing in the soft candlelight. It had been the usual crowded day—the farm, the cattle, the gristmill, sick Indians, complaints from the Cayuses. Narcissa had finished the cooking, washing, the Indian school, the singing, and the Bible reading. She had tucked Alice into bed and sat sewing by the table.

"Narcissa, I need your help on this list," said Marcus. "It's going to the Board with Spalding's letter. I am putting down all that we need for the work of the mission."

"It won't be news to Mr. Greene," said Narcissa. "You have begged him for supplies before, and he always writes that you should do more about saving the souls of the Indians and never mind the hoes and plows. You know how shocked he was when you asked for scalping knives."

Marcus laughed. "Well, it did sound gruesome. How would they know on Beacon Hill, Boston, that a good knife is the basic tool of survival here in the wilderness? But this letter is something special," he went on more seriously. "Mr. Lee is going to Boston, and he has offered to deliver this letter in person. He can tell them the Oregon story. He can tell them what day-by-day living here really means and what it takes to survive in the wilderness."

"Mr. Greene will probably say that the Board is short of funds and the churches are not coming through with the contributions. The same old story." Narcissa sighed wearily.

"I know," added Marcus. "He even objects to my selling beef and corn to the settlers to pay the mission bills at Fort Vancouver. Says it is commercializing Christianity. But Spalding has written a powerful letter," he went on. "You know how vigorously and dramatically he can put things on paper. He placed the responsibility for the success of the mission and the salvation of the Indians squarely up to the Board without mincing words. It should jolt them into action."

"Let's hope it will not offend them but really waken them to the situation," said Narcissa.

For several evenings Marcus and Narcissa worked late, adding essential items, dropping those that might be only convenient, and discussing and determining the exact amount of each that was practical.

When the Spaldings came from Lapwai the letter was read aloud and discussed several times:

After a residence of nearly two years in this country, during which time we have spared no pains . . . we have come to the settled conviction, that you can no longer suffer this great harvest field to remain unoccupied by laborers without inflicting an incalculable injury upon these immortal souls and incurring the fearful displeasure of Heaven. Our reasons are the following. While penning these lines, standing upon these Rocky Mountains, our eyes are upon the unnumbered thousands, standing around us with outstretched hands for help.

As the letter went on it warmed and glowed and led up to the real purpose, an urgent appeal for supplies. Marcus's list of what was needed followed.

The list began with parts for a flour mill and iron for the blacksmith. Then came the human requirements:

To occupy these fields immediately, we ask as the least possible number which God and our conscience will admit us to name:

30 Ordained Ministers	10 physicians and
30 farmers	10 mechanics with their wives
30 school teachers	

Some items taken at random from the long list which followed were:

2000 gun flints (to trade for provisions)	100 scalping knives
50 blankets	4 pitt saw handles with files
50 gross Indian awls	2 cross cut saws handled
	2 broad axes

3 doz. knives and forks of
the most durable kind

4 doz. dining plates

4 doz. breakfast plates

2 doz. chambers with covers

1 Websters Octavo
Dictionary

4 doz. Sab. School Hymn
Books

2 cook stoves

2 brass kettles with bails of
15 gallons

2 sets scrip cards for Inf.
School

2 doz. Parleys Geography

A large supply of plates, cuts of all descriptions, maps, and charts were also requested. "We find Scripture cuts very useful."

The list called up pictures of hard-fisted men using tools, of plain women over cookstoves, of children singing hymns, of a teacher thumbing a dictionary—of toil, hope, faith.

It would probably be two years before they could receive an answer.

Whitman improvised a blacksmith shop. Laboriously he built and operated a gristmill. It ground in a day enough corn to last the mission a week. In the mountains a pitt saw was operated and turned out clean Oregon pine boards that were sledged across fifteen miles to the mission. The big T-shaped mission house was finished and whitewashed with lime made from mussel shells. It was nineteen by forty feet, with an ell twenty-two by thirty, all built of adobe brick. It shone splendidly in the sun and was the pride of the Walla Walla country.

Mr. Edwin O. Hall and his wife arrived from the Sandwich Islands with a wonderful gift from the Owyhee Mission. It was a printing press, which was taken to Lapwai, where Mr. Hall, with an apprentice, printed eight hundred copies of a fifty-two-page book in the Nez Percé language.

On August 23, 1838, the travel-worn "reinforcements" arrived. The party consisted of Mr. Gray, the Reverends Elkanah Walker, Cushing Eells, Asa Bowen and their wives, and Cornelius Rogers as missionary assistant. They had come over the Oregon Trail, most of the way with the fur caravan. The newcomers were all of the Yankee pioneer stock, pious, opinionated, and enduring. Under the grueling hardships of the long trail they had got very much on one another's nerves and had exchanged unchristian revilings. Living in close quarters with the Whitmans did not improve the situation. The atmosphere in Narcissa's kitchen that winter was strained and tense. There were times when she went alone to the river for a good cry.

On December 7 Mrs. Walker gave birth to a fine boy. He was to be the first white American male born in Oregon to reach mature age, and he was christened Cyrus Hamlin Walker.

Eells and Walker explored for a mission site and decided on Tshimakiam, some one hundred and thirty miles to the north. As it was too late in the season to start work on the mission, they returned to Waiilatpu for the winter.

"ROCK OF AGES," SUNDAY, JUNE 23, 1839

It was a lovely morning, and the land was warm and green with June. Alice was bubbling over, for it was her special privilege to select the hymn for morning service. Of all the hymns she and her mother sang together, her favorite was "Rock of Ages." The swinging rhythm of the grand old

hymn drifted across the spring air, and Alice's voice rose
sweet and clear. "She sang it with great clearness and with
such ecstasy as almost to raise her out of her chair." At the
noonday services it was sung again, and mother and daughter joined in its soaring paean.

Sunday afternoon brought to Marcus and Narcissa the
few hours of relaxation that a busy working week afforded.

Husband and I were both engaged in reading. She had just
a few minutes before been reading to her father; had got down
out of his lap, and as my impression, was amusing herself by
the door in the yard. After a few moments, not hearing her
voice, I sent Margaret [an Indian girl] to search for her. She did
not find her readily, and instead of coming to me to tell me she
had not found her, she went to the garden to get some radishes
for supper; on seeing her pass to the water to wash them, I
looked to see if Alice was with her, but saw that she was not.
That moment I began to be alarmed, for Mungo had just been
in and said there were two cups in the river [Alice had earlier
been playing with two cups]. We immediately inquired for her,
but no one had seen her. We then concluded she must be in the
river. We searched down the river, and up and down again in
wild dismay, but could not find her for a long time. Several were
in the river searching far down. By this time we gave her up for
dead. At last an old Indian got into the river where she fell in
and looked along by the shore and found her a short distance
below. But it was too late, she was dead. We made every effort
possible to bring her to life but all was in vain. . . . Previous
to this she had been much afraid to go near the water anywhere,
for her father had once put her in, which so effectually frightened her that we had lost that feeling of anxiety for her in a
measure on its account. But she had gone; yes, and because my
Savior would have it so.

Reaching out for comfort in the darkness, she wrote to her father:

That we loved her most ardently is true, and it is no less true that we feel keenly the severe pangs of separation from her, who was so much the joy and comfort of our hearts in our lonely situation, yet it is the Lord that hath done it and He hath dealt with us as a tender parent deals with the children whom he loves. O, how often have I felt and thought what a privilege it would be, if I could see and unburden to my dear parents the sorrows of my broken and bleeding heart, since we have been bereft of our dear, sweet babe.

The emptiness of her heart she tried to fill with the destitute children that the years brought to her door, until finally she mothered a brood of eleven. She scrubbed and deloused them and patiently subdued the fierce animality that hunger and brutality and destitution had instilled in them, and she fed them with her love.

Jim Bridger sent his little halfbreed daughter, aged six, to Narcissa to be civilized. Later Joe Meek sent to the mission Helen Mar, his six-year-old daughter, to be brought up a Christian. The Indians brought in a half-naked, half-starved child of three, whom Narcissa called David Malin. His Indian mother had left him to die in a pit, and he had been maltreated by the Indian children. "Mother" Whitman opened her heart and her arms and took all these children as her own.

Later, when she had adopted eleven children, she watched her brood closely to prevent them from playing with the Indian children, for they were quick to pick up the Indian tongue and customs and forget the English language and the manners which Narcissa had spent so much time and labor to teach them. This was also true of the Indian students of her school. When they returned to their tribe, all that she had taught them seemed to drop away and be forgotten. Teaching the Indians was a slow and discouraging task, but she never gave up, never wholly despaired, never ceased to pray and have faith that sooner or later every heathen would come to the light of Christianity.

There were lonely nights when Marcus Whitman was away, when Narcissa's thoughts went back to her home and parents, the brothers and sisters together around the beloved fireside; when her heart and eyes flooded with memories of little blue-eyed Alice, and she opened her Bible for the comfort and light that never failed and read: "The eternal God is thy refuge, and underneath are the everlasting arms."

Among the settlers stopping on their way to the Willamette was William Geiger. He was an old friend of Narcissa, from Angelica, New York, and brought messages from dear friends and all the intimate news of the old home. Also among the newcomers were the Reverend J. S. Griffen and Mr. Munger. They were "Free Missionaries," on their own, without support from any congregation. They had no place to go and were something of a problem for Marcus. As Munger was a good mechanic, Marcus hired him to work at the mission. Later he became insane and had to be sent back to the States.

DISCORD, OCTOBER 1840

With the eyes of a frontier farmer, Whitman had looked on Oregon and found the land good. With the faith of the

American pioneer, he believed that this fruitful land was not destined to remain a hunting ground for British fur traders or the French Canadians whose medieval minds could not comprehend the freedom of American democracy. It was not hard for the son of New England pioneers to dream of this land filled with happy families, neat farms, and decent villages and churches. Slowly the vision took shape and obsessed his mind.

To others among the little group of pioneers, the ordeals and privations of the mission brought out all the smallnesses and meannesses of little minds. Narcissa became only too well aware that there were whisperings and complaints, resentment against a man who was too big for them to understand. She well knew that among the women she was spoken of behind her back with sneers and snarls and verbal stabs. The spirit of religion was growing dim among these Christians who so strictly held to the letter. At the annual meeting of the missions it was voted that the Whitmans be asked to remove.

The sudden tragedy of Alice's death shamed this malice for a while. But Spalding again became so vindictive to everyone that some of the missionaries wrote complaints about him back to the Board. The atmosphere became so charged with hatred as to be almost unendurable for Narcissa. For the first time she wrote in her letters home:

My dear husband has suffered more from him in consequence of his wicked jealousy, and his great pique towards me, than can be known in this world. . . . His principal aim has been at me; as he said, "Bring out her character," "Expose her character," as though I was the vilest creature on earth. It is well known I never did anything before I left home to injure

him, and I have done nothing since, and my husband is as
cautious in speaking and thinking evil of him or treating him
unkindly, as my own dear father would be. . . . I never have
had any difficulty with his wife; she has treated me very kindly
to my face, but recently I have learned that she has always
partook of the feelings of her husband. I have always loved her
and felt as if no one could speak against her. . . . Some of
them are writing to the Board and proposing measures to have
an overture and settlement made, and it may require his re-
moval or return to effect it; not so much for his treatment
toward us as some others also.

REHEARSAL FOR A TRAGEDY

Some of the younger Cayuses had been willing to use
the hoe and plow, and their gardens had prospered accordingly. Their children had been the most willing of all,
singing the Christian hymns and some learning to write
and spell out words in the Nez Percé language.

But the older Indians clung to the ancient tribal ways.
They grew jealous as the mission prospered, and grumbled
that they had received no gifts, and demanded payment
for the use of the land, water, wood, and even the air. Whitman patiently explained that he had been asked by the Indians themselves to come and teach them, and had been
offered the use of the land. If the Indians wished him to go
they should vote upon it, and he would act accordingly.

One day an Indian boy ran into the mission and shouted,
"Til-ka-na-ik horses are in the garden eating the corn."
Marcus quickly ordered several Indians to run the horses
out of the gardens. While they were doing this, Til-ka-na-ik
himself appeared and threatened to beat the Indians and

take the mission. He also demanded payment for the land. It was his; he had grown up on it. Whitman said he would not give anything for the land, but that if Til-ka-na-ik wanted to turn his horses in to destroy the garden he might go ahead on his own responsibility. Marcus turned and walked away, leaving the chief baffled and furious by this unexpected nonresistance.

Later a friendly chief asked Marcus why he had let the horses destroy his gardens. Whitman explained what had happened and repeated that he would do nothing in retaliation.

While they were talking Til-ka-na-ik had been listening. He now stepped forward and struck Marcus twice on the chest and ordered him to be still. This demanded instant return in kind, according to the Indian code. Whitman coolly replied that he had been in the habit of talking since childhood and intended to continue.

One morning an Indian named I-a-tin appeared at the mission and said he had come for his son's wages. Whitman had engaged the Indian boy to tend the cattle and horses, but the boy had disappeared and had not been seen at the mission for a month.

"I will pay him when he has served out his time according to our agreement," said Marcus firmly.

"The white doctor treats the Indians badly," muttered the angry Indian.

"It is you who mistreat your white friend," replied Marcus. I-a-tin left angrily, muttering that he would burn the mill if Whitman did not treat him better. The Indians were now trying to provoke the doctor to anger and possibly a fight. These quarrels became contests to see who could best hold his temper. The party that became angry was the one who lost face.

The cook, an Owyhee woman, came to William Gray and said that an Indian was in the kitchen of the old toolhouse, where she was working. This was absolutely against the rules of the station. Gray went at once and told the Indian to leave.

"You think I am a thief?" said the Indian sullenly.

"Tools have been stolen," replied Gray. "If we let one of you in we will have to let in all the Cayuses."

The Indian made an insulting gesture, and Gray hustled him out of the door. The Cayuse went to the corral and roped one of Gray's horses. Gray ran after him, cut the rope, and threw the Indian out of the corral.

That afternoon this same Indian rode up to where Whitman was working. Behind him on the horse was another Indian, apparently his brother. Ignoring Whitman, the Indian attempted to take the same horse out of the corral. More Indians were gathering around.

"If you make yourself a thief how will you cleanse yourself from this sin?" said Whitman mildly.

"It will be good to kill your cattle," shouted the brother savagely.

Til-ka-na-ik had come up now, and more Indians were gathering. Whitman felt he should warn Gray of the danger of this situation at once.

He found Gray working on the roof of the new house. "Let me handle this," he ordered. "You say nothing."

Til-ka-na-ik came forward and said in a bullying tone to Gray, "You must stop this building and leave here tomorrow."

"Tomorrow is the Sabbath," said Whitman sternly. "He cannot go." He turned and walked away. Apparently there was not going to be a fight. Til-ka-na-ik was losing face. He ran after Whitman, excitedly jabbering complaints and accusations that the Indians were not admitted to the mission houses.

Whitman faced about and said, "If you come into our houses and refuse to do as we ask you, it is right for us to put you out!"

His face distorted with rage, the Indian reached out and seized Whitman's ear, giving it a vicious twist. Everyone stood tense, waiting for Whitman to strike back. This would start the fight. Whitman stood perfectly still.

When the Indian let go, Marcus calmly turned his head and offered the other ear. Furiously the enraged chief twisted first one ear and then the other.

Marcus stood calm and cool. It was unbelievable. Nothing like it had ever happened. This was an example of Christian teaching being practiced that was not lost on the Indians.

Til-ka-na-ik snatched off Whitman's hat and threw it in the mud, adding insult to injury. Whitman quietly asked one of the Indians to hand it back to him, and he replaced it on his head. Again the Indian snatched it off and threw it on the ground. Again Marcus motioned to an Indian to pick it up, and put it back on his head, his steady gaze never leaving his tormentor's face.

For the third time the Indian pulled off his hat and threw it into a mud puddle. The hat was in very bad shape when Marcus put it on. In the face of his superb self-control the Indian's fury seemed utterly foolish.

"No doubt you are playing a game," said Marcus contemptuously as he turned and walked away.

Next Sabbath the usual number of friendly Indians appeared at the service. The old chiefs, however, were making speeches against the whites and were forbidding the Indians to help the mission. McKinlay, the new British factor at Walla Walla, had heard of the fracas from both the Indians and Whitman. He immediately sent his interpreter to the Indians with a message saying that any insult offered to the Americans he considered as offered to himself, and that the Indians had conducted themselves like dogs. He added that the Hudson's Bay Company was prepared and determined to avenge any further outrage anywhere at any time.

UNAFRAID

"Marcus," called Narcissa from the kitchen door.

From the tone of her voice Whitman sensed trouble. When he and Gray reached the house he found the kitchen crowded with Indians. It was a place where they were not allowed. He took the Indians into the dining room, locked the kitchen door, and let more Indians in through the regular Indian door.

Marcus could see through the window an Indian brandishing a hammer with which he was signaling to Narcissa to open the kitchen door. It was the troublemaker old Pe-la-is-ti-wat. Sa-ki-aph, his friend, was trying to open the kitchen door from the inside. Whitman called on the chiefs to stop him. There was no response. The Indian had now opened the kitchen door, intending to let in more Indians.

Whitman stepped behind him, gave him a violent shove through the door, and locked it.

Marcus went back to the crowded dining room and sat down. Sa-ki-aph and Pe-la-is-ti-wat began beating on the door with an ax and a hammer. The door burst open, and a horde of Indians rushed in. Narcissa now saw that the house was filled with angry savages.

The two Indians with the hammer and ax were pushing through the crowd to reach Whitman. He called to the chiefs to restore order. Again no answer. Gray and Whitman now grappled with the two savages and twisted the hammer and ax out of their grasp. Instead of striking them down, Whitman merely handed ax and hammer to Gray, who took them upstairs. By naked coolness and courage Marcus was again in control of the situation. Everyone sat down, and the talk began again—but not for long.

Suddenly Sa-ki-aph burst into the room, brandishing a war club, and rushed at Whitman. Marcus leaped up, dodged the blow, and twisted the club from the Indian's hand. Mocking laughter broke out. "You are afraid to die," taunted the chiefs. Whitman vehemently denied it.

At this point Sa-ki-aph came forward with a gun and put the muzzle against Whitman's heart. "Are you not afraid of death?"

Marcus saw Narcissa standing across the room. Her pale face was lifted and her eyes closed. The Indians were shouting, "You are daring us to kill you!"

"No," said Whitman. "I have showed you that I am not afraid to die. But if you commit the crime of murder God will certainly punish you."

The two loyal Owyhees now came in and stood beside

Whitman. This reinforcement had its effect, and the council was resumed.

The Indians demanded to be allowed to enter the mission whenever they wished. Whitman said no; the Indians must obey the mission regulations. Til-ka-na-ik finally burst out in admiration, "It is impossible for us to frighten them. We cannot even bully these white men!"

Here an Indian called Wap-tash-tak-mahl, who had pretended to be friendly, said that it was the custom, whenever a settlement was made, for the whites to give the Indians presents.

"You will never get the value of a single awl or pin from me for your bad conduct. If you want our property for this reason you will have to steal it," replied Marcus sternly.

"That is very hard language," grumbled the Indian.

The Cayuses left the meeting in a sullen mood, saying they were going to Walla Walla to see if McKinlay would repeat his remarks about their being dogs. That night Marcus sent a messenger warning McKinlay.

The next day was the Sabbath. There were no Indians at the service. The sullen Indians hanging about the mission threw stones at the cattle and broke windows. Nonresistance had gone far enough. That night the white men kept guard in the mission with loaded guns. Whitman resolved to leave Waiilatpu and go to Fort Walla Walla till the situation cleared.

On Monday morning a letter came from McKinlay: "I have the pleasure to inform you that there is every prospect of your being allowed to keep peaceful possession of your place and that you will not be further molested by the Indians."

McKinlay had told the Indians that if they harmed the mission he would send word to McLoughlin, who would send many men to take revenge for their crimes. If the Indians apologized for their misdeeds they would probably be forgiven, and the missionaries would not go away but stay and work for their good. The Indians expressed deep contrition for what had passed and made many promises.

THE DESTRUCTIVE ORDER

Those who came over the trail from the States always arrived in the fall. It was September 1842 when a band of white settlers wearily halted at the mission.

Marcus ran out, waving his hat. "Welcome to Waiilatpu. You come as a surprise, but you're mighty welcome," he shouted.

"Pardner," said a dust-covered man, swinging out of the saddle, "I never was so plumb pleased in all my born days to see white folks and houses. The name is Lovejoy. A. L. Lovejoy." He stretched out his hand.

Soon the compound was filled with worn horses and pack mules. "We had to leave the wagons at Snake Fort," Lovejoy explained.

The mission was crowded with women and children. Narcissa was directing groups where to get water and telling them the details for camping. There were one hundred and twelve people in the party, fifty of them men over eighteen. They were mostly Methodists who were stopping over for a couple of days on their way to the Willamette Mission.

That night the Whitmans heard the news of the States from the leader, Dr. Elijah White, and his companion, Mr. Lovejoy. White had been stirring up real interest in Oregon in the big eastern cities. The government had appointed him Sub Indian Agent for Oregon, the first United States officer in the territory. Big things were in the wind.

White delivered the mail to Whitman. Marcus tore open a letter from the Board.

"Something serious?" asked Narcissa, watching his grave face anxiously.

"Yes, listen to this," he said hoarsely, and read:

> Missionary House, Boston
> 25 Feb. 1842

In view of all the circumstances of the mission as presented in letters from your number, the Prudential Committee, on the 23 inst., adopted resolutions—

I. To discontinue the southern branch of the Oregon Mission.

II. To recall the Rev. Henry H. Spalding and wife, with the expectations that they would return to the United States by the earliest suitable opportunity.

III. Transferring Doctor Marcus Whitman and Mr. Cornelius Rogers, if he should be so disposed to continue in the missionary work, to the north branch of the mission.

IV. Appointing Doctor Whitman and Mr. Rogers to dispose of the mission property connected with the south branch of the mission, to the Methodist mission or in such other manner as they might deem advisable. . . .

Whitman immediately summoned the missionaries in from the stations and read the letter to them. The men looked gloomily at one another. In the face of this their quarrels and backbiting seemed suddenly insignificant.

They exchanged apologies. There were reconciliations and exchanges of good will and promises of no further malice. But what were they to do now in the face of "the Destructive Order"?

Was this to be the end, the end of all their labor, efforts, building? In the six years since they had come, their roots had sunk deep into the land. All they had sown was now to be uprooted. Whitman wrote to the Board reporting the reconciliation that had taken place between the quarreling members at the last annual meeting; that now they were all united in spirit again. It would be months before the letter arrived. Surely then the Board would rescind the destructive resolution. But all was uncertain.

"Letters take too long, back and forth. Someone must go in person and explain to the Board," burst out Marcus.

"But the mountains are impassable in winter. It is madness. It is suicide," replied the others. As Whitman argued for his project he became more resolute. If he started now —early October—he could cross before the snow blocked the passes, and reach St. Louis by Christmas.

Before the meeting adjourned they had passed a resolution:

Resolved, That if arrangements can be made to continue the operations of this station, that Dr. Marcus Whitman be at liberty and advised to visit the United States as soon as practicable, to confer with the Committee of the A. B. C. F. M. in regard to the interest of this Mission.

(Signed)   E. Walker, Moderator

        Cushing Eells, Scribe

        H. H. Spalding

Waiilatpu, Sep. 28, 1842

Suddenly Marcus realized that something more than saving the mission was in his mind. Here was his opportunity to help gain Oregon. Here was the answer. He would go to Washington, see the politicians, the President, tell them about Oregon, show them that now was the time to act, to claim the land for the United States before it was too late. It had all been leading up to this, all he had been and done had prepared him for this moment. This was his wider mission and larger purpose.

As he explained to Narcissa it all seemed plain. In his enthusiasm the journey across the mountains, to St. Louis, seemed a mere detail. The opposition of reluctant senators would melt; the willing aid of President Tyler seemed certain.

"But you cannot go alone, you must have a companion," pleaded Narcissa. But who? None of the missionaries could leave their posts without orders from the Board. This was Friday, and he planned to leave the following Monday, October 3. Every day counted if he was to cross the mountains before snow.

Narcissa understood Marcus too well to think of herself, of the anxious months alone, waiting, hoping, fighting despair. Cheerfully she helped through the remaining days of hectic preparation. Marcus invited Mr. Lovejoy to make the trip with him. Surprisingly, Lovejoy considered and accepted. "He has for a companion Mr. Lovejoy, a respectable, intelligent man and a lawyer, but not a Christian, who expects to accompany him all the way to Boston, as his friends are in that region, and perhaps to Washington," wrote Narcissa. Whatever Mr. Lovejoy may have lacked as an orthodox Christian, he must certainly have loved to travel, for he had just come some three thousand miles across the continent, and now he was willing to repeat the hazardous journey.

It was on October 3, 1842, that Marcus and Lovejoy started on their journey. As the two men rode away Narcissa stood in the doorway with her chin up, smiling and waving. After they had gone she went to her room alone to pray. There on the table were Marcus's forgotten compass, pencil, and comb. However would he comb his hair on all the long journey? What would he look like when he got to Washington, all uncombed? What would the President think of him? The trifling worry busied her thought, focusing it on the concrete and keeping her from sinking into dark and vague forebodings of tomorrow.

ALONE, OCTOBER 1842

A halo of yellow light about the candle flame accented the darkness of the room. The darkness closed around Narcissa with an almost solid pressure. It was a darkness of the spirit in which all hope and light seemed lost in black forebodings. "And the darkness he called night." She had spent many a lonely night before at the mission when the doctor was away on sick calls. But now he had gone for at least a year; she did not know when, if ever, he would return. The void was filling with formless shapes of terror.

She opened her Bible. "He shall cover thee with his feathers, and under his wings shalt thou trust; his truth shall be thy shield and buckler. Thou shalt not be afraid for the terror by night; nor for the arrow that flieth by day." She closed the book and blew out the candle.

About midnight I was awakened by someone trying to open my bedroom door. At first I did not know what to understand by it. I raised my head and listened awhile and then lay down again. Soon the latch was raised and the door opened a little. I sprang from the bed in a moment and closed the door again, but the ruffian pushed and pushed and tried to unlatch it, but could not succeed; finally he gained upon me until he opened the door again and as I suppose disengaged his blanket (at the same time I calling John) and ran as for his life. The east dining room was open. I thought it was locked, but it appears that it was not. I fastened the door, lit a candle and went to bed trembling and cold, but could not rest until I had called John (a Hawaian) to bring his bed and sleep in the kitchen. It was in such a time that I found he was too far off. Had the ruffian persisted I do not know what I should have done. I did not think of the war club, but I thought of the poker. Thanks be to our Heavenly Father. He mercifully delivered me from the hand of a savage man.

Next morning Narcissa told the story to the two Indians, Feathercap and McKay. "I came near beating him," added Narcissa sternly, trying to look ferocious. "That would have been good," said Feathercap gravely. "Then we should have known who he was."

Next day the news reached Fort Walla Walla. The factor McKinlay had been planning to ride over with his wife to see how Narcissa was doing. Now he came in a wagon and said she must come to stay at the fort. Waiilatpu was not safe for a woman alone. The Indians wanted her to stay, and she herself had clung loyally to the mission. But she knew that Mr. Geiger had agreed to take charge of the mission until Whitman should return. Geiger got on well with the Indians, and so Narcissa rode back to Walla Walla, lying exhausted in the wagon bed.

A few days later came news that the gristmill had been burned in the night, with two hundred bushels of precious grain. The fire was evidently the work of malicious Indians.

"My poor husband will feel this sadly," said Narcissa. "So much lost, and so much too that will save labor. I think, sometimes, if I had not left perhaps it would not have been burned."

THE LONELY WINTER, 1842–1843

Narcissa left the mission children at Walla Walla and, taking only the two girls, little Mary Anne Bridger and Helen Mar Meek, went down the Columbia to spend the winter visiting old friends at the Dalles, Vancouver, and on the Willamette. She was free of the back-breaking domestic labors of the mission, but she was lonely, anxious, and at times depressed. Her health was bad.

From the Dalles Mission (called Waskopum), halfway down the Columbia, she wrote, "Notwithstanding all our adversities I have no occasion to feel the least regret that Husband has gone and left me here—the cause demanded it increasingly so every hour."

Existing in the wilderness required constant alertness in the practice of those skills by which men lived. A slip of the hand or foot could send a canoe out into the current above the falls of the Willamette. Six people were drowned that winter in just such an accident. Among them was Narcissa's friend Cornelius Rogers and his wife with her little sister. This made sad news along the river.

All the talk that winter among the tribes of the Columbia was of war. The Indians had heard that the Americans were coming to make war upon them, that Whitman was bringing soldiers from the East. The Indians were troubled over these rumors. The agent Elijah White had been trying to persuade them to adopt a set of laws he had arbitrarily drawn up, and they were unwilling to do this.

Spring came. Perhaps Marcus was starting back. Narcissa did not know. Her letters to him might be addressed to the dead instead of to the living. She refused the dark suggestion. When he came they would start again. The yearning to save the souls of the Indians possessed her. They would go on together with the great work at Waiilatpu.

In the spring of 1843 the persuasive White, together with Spalding and Narcissa, met the Oregon tribes at the Dalles for a powwow. All went well, and the whole party, including three hundred Nez Percés, returned to Waiilatpu.

To their amazement they found three hundred mounted Walla Walla and Cayuse Indians on the open ground in front of the mission. For an unpleasant hour it looked as if there would be a fight, until Mr. Spalding called everyone to attend a religious service he was holding. This cooled off the atmosphere. For the next four days there were Indian councils and speeches and peaceful agreements. The Indians were given a cow for each horse that Jason Lee had taken, and so an old score was settled. The council wound up with a grand two-day feast and barbecue. Dr. White contributed an ox, and Narcissa presented one of the Whitman hogs.

The Cayuses told Geiger that it was said the whites in

the Willamette Mission intended to attack them and take away their land. The young braves were for attacking the Willamette first, but the old men had said they should wait and find out the truth. Yellow Serpent, the Walla Walla chief, had gone to Vancouver and counciled with Mc-Loughlin, the great white chief, who said, "Indians should have no fear, but all should keep the peace." Geiger urged them to be calm and to cultivate their ground, raise more crops, so that there would be plenty of food.

There were long lonely months when the lights of the little missions of the Oregon wilderness seemed to shine dimly in a wasteland where the heathen sat in darkness. At such times Narcissa's thoughts went longingly back to the home fireside in New York State, where she saw Marcus among her dear family and friends. There were black hours when she wondered if she would ever see any of them again.

Then, as she prayed, the old hopes and buoyancy revived. Marcus was surely coming back with more laborers for the vineyards of the Lord. They would start together again in the great work still remaining, of bringing the light of Christ's salvation to the people that sat in that land of the shadow of death.

As the time approached for the arrival of the immigrant train, she went up the Columbia to the friendly Methodist mission near the Dalles. Here she waited longingly for the day when Marcus would come.

PART THREE
THE GREAT MIGRATION

THE WHITE TOPS

Ho there, you movers with the restless feet, are you going to Oregon?
Come, let us start up the Missouri and along the Platte westward.
Fall in line, forward the caravan, let the wheels roll.
Take only your plows and Bibles, your rifles and blankets,
Leaving all else, the junk of the past, the old bonds and chains,
The gray yesterdays, the old routines, the trimmed lawns.
Tonight we camp under the stars; the horse guard leans on his rifle.
By the campfires we sing the old songs—"Rock of Ages, Truth divine."
Lightfoot the dancers swing to "Oh, Susanna."
Tomorrow a fresh start, the bugle sounds. Rise up! Rise up!
Fall in line! The bull whips crack, the teamsters shout.
Wagons west, forward the caravan, let the wheels roll.
Forward the white tops on the Oregon Trail, on to the Columbia.

A Noble Pioneer We Judge Him to Be
The *Daily Tribune* Office, New York, March 1843

"I would like to see Mr. Horace Greeley," said the stranger, taking off his shabby fur cap.

"Who shall I say is calling?" asked the secretary without looking up from the desk.

"Doctor Marcus Whitman, of Oregon," said the quiet voice.

"Of where?" asked the startled secretary, looking up in amazement at the strange figure before him.

"Oregon," repeated the doctor, leaning over the desk.

With a warm greeting Mr. Greeley seated his guest in

the cluttered editorial office. Glancing with some curiosity at the strange figure before him, he noted the fur cap, the shabby buffalo coat, and the shrunken buckskins that revealed the muscular figure beneath. At this time, in Mr. Greeley's opinion, people who went to Oregon were definitely insane; the evidence before him suggested that this was so.

Mr. Greeley himself was somewhat of an eccentric, with his droll manners, his old white hat and coat, his linen pants stuffed in his boot tops, and his great round face fringed with yellow chinwhiskers. But his bold editorials championing popular and unpopular causes had made a large circulation for his *Daily Tribune* throughout the country.

The doctor's story was amazing. It was also first-hand news of Oregon. His hazardous winter journey across the mountains and the Santa Fe trail to St. Louis was unprecedented. And why had he made the perilous journey?

Marcus now launched into his great theme. He wanted to take a great wagon train of emigrants to Oregon this spring. Would Mr. Greeley urge his readers to go?

Marcus also told of his visit to Washington. He had seen Mr. Daniel Webster, who was not interested because he planned to trade Oregon to Britain for the Newfoundland fisheries, which some of his constituents wanted the United States to acquire. Marcus had persisted. Through his friend Senator Linn of Missouri he had been able to see President Tyler. The President had assured him that if he could open a wagon road to Oregon by leading an emigrant wagon train across the mountains within the next year, the President would withhold any action that would give the Oregon territory to the British. Whitman was greatly encouraged by this. He was now on his way to Boston to see the American Board. Everywhere he urged people to go to Oregon.

Mr. Greeley was not enthusiastic, but, as he saw that this was an earnest man, even a noble one, and a worthy Christian missionary, he reported his interview with Whitman to the readers of the *Tribune:*

A slight glance at him when he entered our office would convince anyone that he had seen all the hardships of a life in the wilderness.

A noble pioneer we judge him to be, a man fitted to be chief in rearing a moral empire among the wild men of the wilderness.

A VISIT TO BEACON HILL

People smiled and looked after him as he passed along the streets of New York and Boston. He might have come from Mars or the moon, so odd and foreign seemed this stranger from the West. Not that he wanted to be conspicuous. He simply did not have the money to buy a fashionable outfit, so he wore the worn buffalo coat, fur cap, and leather pants in which he had ridden across America.

The crowds of people confused him. They got in his way, and he in theirs. In the streets he struggled against a tide of pale-faced masks. In the crowds he was more desperately lonely than on the wilderness trails of Oregon. He was weary of talking to paunchy men in swivel chairs who did not understand. For the first time he realized how completely he belonged to Oregon, to the Columbia, to Waiilatpu.

It was on March 30, 1843, that he stalked into the offices of the American Board on Beacon Hill, Boston, causing severe shock to that well-regulated body.

"What are you here for, leaving your post?" barked Mr. Hill, the treasurer. "Don't you know it's strictly against regulations for a missionary to leave his post without orders from the Board?" After giving the doctor a brisk reprimand he counted out some money, saying, "Here, go and get some clothes."

A few days later Marcus, arrayed in an uncomfortable suit of new clothes, appeared before the outraged Prudential Committee. When he had finished his epic story the committee sat silent in the presence of a great man's sincerity and devotion. Then they, of course, passed a resolution:

Resolved, That Doctor Marcus Whitman and Rev. H. H. Spalding be authorized to continue to occupy the stations of Waiilatpu and Clearwater, as they did previous to the adoption of the resolution referred to above.

To Whitman's urgent request that Christian families of farmers be sent to locations near the missions, they cautiously replied:

Resolved, That a missionary be sent to strengthen the Oregon Mission, if a suitable person can be obtained.

In Boston, Marcus could find no lay helpers willing to go to Oregon, but he was still hopeful.

Spring was at hand. With immense relief he again turned west, stopping to visit his aged parents and old friends in Rushville, New York. Of course he also sought out Father and Mother Prentiss. They sat late into the night as he gave them Narcissa's messages and told them of her courage and faith and love.

Marcus realized that though he and Narcissa now belonged to the West they were still of the East too. The roots and ties of affection and memory bound East and West together. Americans could never be divided. Some day the great wilderness that separated East and West would be filled with one people, and their sons and daughters would grow up, like the green corn, into a mighty nation, one and indivisible.

He was taking back to Oregon with him at least one new recruit. This was his thirteen-year-old nephew, Perrin Whitman. Together they had pleaded with the family and had won. The boy was a quick and eager learner, anxious to ride west with his hero uncle on the great adventure.

SHOVING OFF FROM INDEPENDENCE, MISSOURI
MAY 1843

The May sunshine was drying out the flooded land and the seas of mud that covered the lowlands. The landscape was green with new grass. Until the grass came, western travelers could not feed their horses and cattle on the prairie.

The wagons of the great emigration were being readied. Two thousand animals—horses, oxen, mules, milch cows —covered the plain. Their lowing and heehawing made a raucous chorus. When the final count of the emigrants was taken there were 295 men over sixteen years of age who could handle a rifle. The others, including women and children, numbered 875. One hundred and eleven wagons of various shapes and sizes, covered with canvas for protection against the sun and rain, were loaded with the fixings and paraphernalia of a people on the march.

Some of the wagons had already started. Before Whitman had been in Independence a week he was the center of committees and groups asking questions about routes, directions, equipment, fords, and how to order the march of the great caravan. Would it be safe to divide into two columns through the Indian country? Marcus said it would be best to march in two parallel columns. He ended by repeating: "Travel, travel, travel, nothing else will take you to the end of your journey; nothing is wise that does not help you along; nothing is good for you that causes a moment's delay."

Before dawn the camp was alive with activity. Teams were harnessed and the first wagons began to move. Others fell in line until, by sunup, the train was rolling; the daily routine of the prairie march had begun. They moved at an average rate of fifteen miles a day, sometimes more, less when there were rivers to ford. The Big Blue was the first crossing, and the doctor rode across in advance, finding firm bottom where the water was shallow.

At nightfall the wagons formed in a great circle, the campfires were lighted, the cattle bedded down for the night, and the guard set.

Across the level plains in the July heat they followed the south shore of the Platte, the river that was said to flow upside down because so much of the water ran under the quicksands of its shallow channel. They followed its course westward. The travelers paused to gawk in wonder at the prairie landmarks—Scotts Bluff, Courthouse Rock, and the tall pinnacle of Chimney Rock.

ACROSS THE PLAINS

The dark lifts along the east. The red disk of the sun rises against the black edge of the prairie. The sentinels fire their rifles. It is the "wake up" signal. Sixty teamsters roll out of their blankets, pull on their boots, and round up the cattle herd on the prairie beyond the circle of wagons.

The women are up. The smell of frying pork fills the air, and the smoke from the campfires rises in a hundred tall columns. Each driver by now has his ox or mule team harnessed. Breakfast is bolted, tents are struck, and the camp duffel is loaded in the wagons.

The drivers shout, the bull whips crack. At exactly seven the starting bugle sounds across the prairie. The massive oxen throw their weight against the yokes, the mules strain in their harnesses, the creaking wheels turn, and each wagon falls into place in the long line. Slowly they move out over the plain in two long parallel columns.

Fifteen or so young hunters on swift horses ride off to look for buffalo. The pilot rides well ahead. He carries in his memory a perfect map of valleys and rivers, for he has been an Ashley man, a mountain man. He wears fringed buckskins; his long hair, falling on his shoulders, frames his dark face. He is indistinguishable from an Indian.

Little girls in pigtails peer over the tailboards of the wagons. Small freckled-faced boys sit proudly on the driver's seat beside the teamster, or trot with the hound dogs beside their daddies by the lead ox teams. Under the wagon hoods the sunbonneted women sit among the baggage, nursing their babies. They sing and gossip and talk woman-talk. Young wives listen to grandmothers' lore.

Climbing the naked sky, the sun, a white ball of fire, scorches the prairie with shimmering waves of heat. The cow column follows in the dust behind the wagons. Five hours drop behind. The pilot signals for the noon halt. The wagons draw up, four abreast. The teams are loosed but not unyoked. They drink eagerly from the water pits dug in the sand by the Platte. Families sit in the narrow shadow of the wagons, silently chewing the midday meal. At one o'clock the wagons re-form, and the train starts on the long afternoon haul. The teamsters drowse. The women in the wagons fall asleep. The wagon wheels complain for grease, and the cattle blow the alkali dust impatiently from their nostrils.

The sun is dropping down the vast empty ocean of the sky. The pilot, well ahead, has found a campsite with water and grass. The great ball of the sun turns red on the edge of the west; little cloud processions parade along the horizon. The wagons wheel and come to a stop, tongue to tailboard, until the great protecting circle is complete. The cattle are driven out to grass on the prairie. The guards are stationed. In the great compound the cookfires of buffalo chips are started. The good smell of coffee spreads around. If the hunters have brought in meat it is divided equally among the platoons of four wagons each. Now the women take over. Dough is fried in the buffalo fat for "prairie bread." A thousand husky feeders sit about the campfires, champing their jaws. The prairie earth is dining table, chairs, and bed.

There is laughter and banter on full stomachs. How about a song, a river chantey or a mountain ballad? Another group is pious, and the grand harmonies of "Rock of Ages" rise to the stars. A fiddle strikes up a teasing jig, and feet begin to stomp and swing. The fires die down. In the wagons, in tents, and under the open sky, snorers tune up under their blankets. Out on the prairie the wolf howls rise, quavering and mournful across the dark. The Great Migration is asleep.

ACROSS THE GREAT DIVIDE

Whitman was active day and night. When a wagon dropped out of line, the doctor stopped, pitched a tent, and started a fire. A few hours later the wagon would overtake the train, with the mother and a new baby and the doctor looking very pleased. There were accidents and tragedies, though the doctor did what he could. "We buried a small boy this morning that died from a wagon having passed over his abdomen." Births, accidents, sickness, death, overtook but never stopped the emigrant train.

Through dusty days and hot weeks the columns steadily advanced. Water and grass were the vital necessities. The pilot and his scouts planned to reach water and grass at the end of each day's march.

At Fort Laramie the Laramie River was on the rampage from the melting mountain snows and could not be forded. The wagon beds were detached from the wheel-carriages to be used as boats, but first a guide line had to be taken across the river. Nobody offered to swim the cold torrent with the line.

"Give me the rope," called out Marcus. He tied it round his waist and urged his horse into the water. The current had carried him far downstream before he reached the opposite shore. The wagon beds were ferried back and forth until all the baggage and the women and children were safely across.

It was seven years since Marcus and Narcissa had camped under the walls of Fort Laramie. "God's angels watch over her now," he prayed.

Again the campfires gleamed on the prairie about the fort, and the emigrants rested and did the family washing. The caravans now pushed up the Platte, past Independence Rock, where they left a few hundred more autographs on that famous prairie register, and came through the wild gorge of Devil Gate. Crossing the level sagebrush desert, they were hardly aware that they were in the great South Pass. Just beyond, they came upon Pacific Springs, where they drank the first westward-running water and sang hosannas.

As the caravans camped on the great Continental Divide at the South Pass the pioneers were exuberant, believing that they had reached the gates of Oregon. Few of them realized that a thousand miles of the roughest wayfaring in America still lay before them. The two caravans now broke up into small parties to find their tortuous way through the heart of the Rockies to Fort Hall. There the final test of their purpose to take wagons across the mountains to the Columbia would come. No wagon train had ever gone beyond Fort Hall.

Slowly the small bands of wagons wound across the Green River Valley. Whitman was guiding them over the

route he had followed with McKay and McLeod. At Hams
Fork they turned northward to cross the Bear River. Skirt-
ing the northern end of the Wasatch range, among towering peaks, they found the Soda Springs, where the water
bubbled up in a strange effervescence. They were in the
heart of the country of the mountain men. Fifty more miles
of rugged travel would bring them to Fort Hall.

THE KEY TO OREGON
FORT HALL, SEPTEMBER 1843

The weary travelers camped in the clearing that surrounded the Hudson's Bay Company's grim little fort on
the banks of the Snake where the great river rushed westward past its bastions in a great twisting thousand-mile S
to join the mighty Columbia. Over a hundred great wagons
under the walls made a spectacle the fort had never before
witnessed.

Seven years before, Marcus had dragged his cart—sometimes upside down—from Fort Hall to Snake Fort on the
Boise River. He was certain that others could take their
wagons and women on to the Columbia. These families
now at Fort Hall could do it with their wagons right side
up. To leave the wagons here would be to abandon the
whole expedition. The baggage of a thousand emigrants
could not be packed on horseback and muleback through
the canyons of the Snake and over the steep backs of the
Blue Mountains.

"You can make it with the wagons! Stick to the wagons!
You will need those oxen to plow the valleys of the Willamette, to start your herds of cattle on the grasslands,"

Whitman repeated over and over. "It is a well-known fact that two years ago four men were able to take three wagons on to the Walla Walla," he added.

In the fort, bewildered Missourians crowded into the commandant's office to listen to the advice of Captain Grant. The Britisher pointed out that all previous expeditions had left their wagons at the fort. He was of the opinion that no wagons would ever reach the Columbia. Even if the Americans attempted it with packhorses they would find no food or game on the way. They would starve to death in the attempt, he assured them cheerfully. Recently he had heard that the Indians were plotting to attack the Americans on the way to the Columbia. Why go to a desert like Oregon anyway, when they could go by a short easy route to bountiful California?

Perrin Whitman listened carefully to these arguments and reported them to his Uncle Marcus. "Oh, Uncle Marcus, and do you know what I heard him say after the Americans had left? He said, 'I would not say it was impossible for them to take the wagons through, for if the Americans took the notion to do it I believe they could remove Mount Hood!' "

The emigrants were now ready to make their decision by vote in the usual democratic way, with arguing and discussion and everybody having his say and putting in his two cents' worth. Captain Grant's remarks had sunk in. Some thought they made a lot of sense. There were complainers and whiners who said that the doctor had brought the whole caboodle to ruination.

"Shut up and listen to Doc Whitman," the crowd shouted.

Marcus rose and said simply, "Stick to your wagons and oxen. You'll need them when you start farming in the Willamette. Farther on at Snake Fort I can show you the wagon I brought there myself. Others have made this trip, and you can too. If we all pull together we can haul the wagons through in spite of hell and high water. I've never let any of you down yet, and I never will. If we get through this year, more will come next year. Soon there will be thousands more with cattle, sheep, and hogs as well. We have never turned back yet, and we are not going to turn back now!" He ended by telling them Grant's remark about the Americans moving Mount Hood if they took the notion to.

There were wild whoops and cheers when he finished, and shouts of "On to the Columbia! Stick to the wagons! Oregon for the Americans!"

These Yankees, Kentucks, Buckeyes, Tar Heels, Illinoisans, Missourians, were not the breeds ever to turn back, any more than their fathers had turned back coming through Cumberland Gap over the Wilderness Road, or rafting down the Ohio; any more than their tough ancestors had turned back at Concord Bridge or Bunker Hill or when the *Mayflower* had set sail from New Plymouth back to old England. Their toes had been turned west for so long that it seemed they just couldn't point any other way!

Next morning the wagons were rolling down the south bank of the Snake, and the tireless tune of "Oh, Susanna" twanged and echoed in the canyons. They would ford the Snake at Glenn's Ferry, cross over to the north bank, and make their way across country to Snake Fort (later called

Fort Boise) on the Boise River. Following this stream would again take them to the Snake. Their route was across some of the roughest country on the continent.

Crossing the Snake

The Snake was deep, wide, and swift. The wagons had crossed all kinds of rivers in different ways, but this river was the toughest customer they had yet met.

The wagon teams formed a line and were chained together. In front and in the rear the strongest teams were set as anchors.

Marcus tied a rope around his waist and rode into the river. The swift current carried his horse far downstream. The crowd along the bank anxiously watched the speck of man and horse as it moved across the rushing torrent. As they clambered out on the other side a cheer went up. "He made it!" Now half a dozen young men on horses tied their ropes to the lead team.

"All ready?" yelled the leader.

"Yeah," went down the line.

"Let 'er go-o-o-o!" he bawled.

The whips cracked, the drivers yelled. Horses, mules, oxen strained. The train pitched forward down the bank and into the water. The current swept the lead wagons in a long curve downstream. When the leading horsemen had again found bottom Whitman shouted, "Now, all together-r-r-r-r!"

The horses strained back on their haunches, and their forehoofs sank in the earth as the towlines straightened taut against the full force of the current. Slowly the head of the train began to pull upstream. The drivers cracked their bull whips and shouted wildly. The rushing water piled up against the long curved barrier of the wagons. By now the lead teams had found footing on the far side and were heaving the great wagons up the opposite bank. It was a superb maneuver, a beautiful piece of coordinated action perfectly carried out.

When the last wagon had been hauled out, the doctor, turning back, saw an ox team that had undertaken to cross alone struggling upstream only a few yards above the rapids. The exhausted oxen had come to a standstill. The doctor dashed down the bank, rode into the river, and swung his rope across to the teamster, who tied it to the leading ox. As horse and rider threw their weight on the line it gave just enough anchorage for the straining oxen to overcome the force of the current and pull out. "Better stick with us next time," called the doctor cheerily as the teamster shouted his thanks.

The train re-formed and struck out on the rough trail for the Boise River.

THE LAST MILES ARE THE HARDEST

At Snake Fort, as it was then called, the wagon train halted to catch its breath for the final push to the Columbia, two hundred and fifty miles away. The terrific ordeal of the wagons had toughened some of the families so that they had an unshakable confidence. Others had been worn down and grown dispirited, irritable, and vicious-tempered.

At the fort, Marcus found his old two-wheeled cart as

stout as ever. He showed it with pride and told of the comical upsets of his first journey. Here he also found a relief party of Cayuse Indians from Waiilatpu with four pack horses loaded with flour. They had been sent by Geiger to meet the emigration. They brought a letter from Mr. Walker. Would the doctor come to Lapwai as soon as possible? Spalding and Eliza were both desperately ill. The doctor never failed such a call. He decided to drive ahead with a party of five men in a light wagon. Its tracks would be a guide for the wagon train. He engaged an old chief named Istakus, who could not speak a word of English, to guide the wagon train. The Indian sign language was perfectly understood by the pilots.

In five days (on September 25) Marcus reached Lapwai and found that the Spaldings were out of danger and on the way to recovery. Next day he started for Waiilatpu with Geiger, who had come to meet him. From there he planned to go down the Columbia to meet Narcissa, hoping to find her at the Dalles, the halfway station on the Columbia.

At Waiilatpu he found that the mission house had been broken into by some horsemen riding in advance of the emigrant train. This did not seem like gratitude for his services. But everything else was in good order, and there had been fine crops under Geiger's faithful management. He viewed the burned gristmill and planned to rebuild it. After one day's rest he started across the wilderness in answer to a professional call from Mrs. Eells at Tshimakain, 180 miles away, and arrived in time to deliver her baby. He started back the same afternoon and reached

Waiilatpu in time to furnish supplies and aid to the emigrant train, which was now passing on its way to the Dalles.

At last he was free. He was soon speeding down the Columbia toward the Dalles and Narcissa. As he came up the trail from the river, she ran to meet him and threw herself into his arms. He noted with a pang how thin and worn was her face. But her eyes glowed with the old light when he gave her the messages of affection from her family and the old friends at Rushville, and all the details about each one of them. She listened earnestly as he went on to tell of his visits to Washington, New York, and Boston, and of his adventures on the long trek east and west. Briefly she recounted her lonely vigils and her ill health, and gave him details of the Indian unrest and of the complaints of the various chieftains whose grievances he knew so well. At once they began to make plans.

They would have to start all over again. There would be more difficult tasks. The weary, the naked, the hungry would come to their door, seeking food and comfort. There was still time to persuade the Indians to farm their lands, to lay down the tomahawk and take up the hoe and the plow.

They might have gone back to the East with honor, to comfort and success, for they were still young. Only they never thought of it. They were builders, crusaders, and pioneers who never turned back on the trail. And so they again came to Waiilatpu, the place of rye grass, where stood the stout cabins of the mission they had built with their own hands. This was home, the dearest place on earth.

Several weeks after the emigrant train had reached the Columbia, a column of United States Cavalry rode into Waiilatpu under the command of Colonel John Charles Frémont. He had been sent by the President to protect the emigrant train from the Indians along the way. As he was known as "the pathfinder," he could not have got lost, but he had never been seen by the emigrant train on the long journey.

It was not the Army, not Congress or the President, that opened the trail to Oregon, but the will of a free people. They had not waited for the politicians, the statesmen, the soldiers, or the diplomats, but had loaded their wagons and started them rolling westward.

Marcus knew well enough that no one man alone could "save" Oregon for the United States, but he had done his part. While others had delayed or opposed or said it was not worth doing, he had acted.

He had seen the vision of the continental nation, and he had helped to open the way.

PART FOUR
THE BROKEN SONG

To my mind all my work and plans involved
Time and Distance and required confidence in
the stability of God's purpose to have the utter-
most part of the Earth for His possession.

—MARCUS WHITMAN

WOMEN OF THE WAGONS

Women of the wagons under the faded sunbonnets,
Forsaking the easier ways, the comforts, the securities,
For the long trek over the alkali deserts, walking by the ox teams,
Bending over the campfires, cookstoves, the washtubs.

Makers of homes in lonely cabins and sod huts,
Crooning the cradle songs, watchers by bedsides, weepers by graves,
No whimpering, no whining, when the going was rough,
Only grateful that the children were safe and the men came through
*   sound and whole.*

Keepers of the faith, the kingdom made without hands,
Making the wilderness to blossom, making the decent villages,
The schools, the churches, the democratic community
With the free ballot, the private individual choice.

Misshapen hands and bodies worn with hard labor,
Faces weathered by sun and wind and carved by the years,
Beautiful beyond the mere flesh, women clothed with the sun,
Women of the wagons under the faded sunbonnets.

Starting Again, 1843–1844

There it lay before them, the T-shaped mission house, the mansion and the blacksmith shop and the storehouses, fringed by the cottonwoods and willows along the river. Beyond was the distant blue wall of the mountains. All had been bought with a price—the toil, the tears, and now the victory.

It was almost like starting over again, except there were the buildings in good shape, and the land lay ready and sweet for the seed. Mr. Geiger had been a faithful steward in their absence.

The ordeal had left its marks. The doctor was lame from a bone tumor in his foot, but he went cheerfully about his

125

work on crutches. Narcissa had been ill much of the time during Marcus's absence, and since his return she had been several times near the point of death. But now they were home, and with the new plans, the old incurable buoyancy surged up in her heart, and her health and strength increased daily.

The migration had stripped the mission of all food except potatoes. That winter these were their principal food. Six exhausted families and several bachelors from the migration had stopped for the winter at the mission. The doctor had delivered three new babies, and his sick patients were coming on well. Getting the mission going brought unending work, but Marcus thrived on it, and Narcissa's health improved.

As dazed and exhausted men from the East resting at the mission came back to health and strength, the doctor found that among them were craftsmen and mechanics whose skills he needed. He soon found he had a blacksmith, a wheelwright, a chairmaker, a millwright, and a hatter! He found work for them all, for everything at the station had to be made by hand.

Narcissa too found she had helpers. Women and children of the families who were spending the winter lent a hand. She started classes in sewing and reading and Bible lessons. There were regular Sunday services and children's classes. Mr. Geiger had a knack with children and made an excellent teacher.

Late in February the Indians came back from the Grande Ronde and flocked to the Sunday services. Sometimes there were as many as two or three hundred dark faces listening intently to Perrin's Bible reading in the

Nez Percé language. He had picked up the strange tongue quickly and was soon able to speak it better than Uncle Marcus.

Perrin would soon be fifteen years old. This pioneer life was exciting, and he took to it with zest. Under Uncle Marcus's watchful eye he was learning to take a man's part in the rough frontier way of life in this lawless land where a boy had to learn quickly.

The doctor knew that each year would bring more immigrants, that the Indians were doomed unless they could learn the white man's ways with the plow and the hoe. It would not be long before neither Indians nor whites would want or need a foreign mission in Oregon. His mission work was nearly done. Marcus thought about retiring when this time came.

THE MIGRATION OF 1844

The mission was now a way station on the Oregon Trail. That spring the plows again turned the good earth, and every foot of soil was planted with crops and garden. They must be ready for the immigrants who would be arriving in the fall.

A new gristmill must be built. With the help of the millwright and the blacksmith, Marcus contrived a mill with two forty-inch granite grindstones and a horizontal water wheel. It was a crazy machine, but it worked. It ground corn and wheat! He had seventeen beeves, and the hundred ewes would bear two hundred lambs this year. His letters to Mr. Greene were full of the wonders of Oregon. He urged that strong New England families come to this land of plenty, where every man was given one square mile (640 acres) wherever he might choose, where the dry grass lasted until the spring green, and cattle fed on the range all through the mild winter. He urged that the Board send another ordained minister of the gospel.

He wrote Mr. Greene that he needed a carding machine for the wool of his sheep. Oregon needed pioneers in the wool industry. He sent a list of books that were needed for doctors and for students for the ministry.

That fall the crops were abundant, and the sound of the grinding mill wheels filled the air. The outriders of the annual migration arrived with news that fifteen hundred emigrants, toiling through the mountains in little bands, were strung out all along the rough trail from Fort Hall.

The most prosperous families with the strongest wagons kept on to the Dalles. Some occasionally stopped at the mission to buy flour and the mission beef. Marcus trusted many of them to pay him, and of the destitute he asked no money.

Later came the stragglers, ragged and hungry, with their sick. There were broken men stricken unto death, and weary women heavy with child. The mission became a hospital and a maternity ward and a soup kitchen. Narcissa watched late into the night by the bedsides of dying men and comforted and fed the hollow-cheeked children, and the doctor delivered babies and tended the sick. Narcissa wrote: "We need many houses to accommodate the families that will be obliged to winter here. All the house room that we have to spare is filled already. It is expected that there are more than five hundred souls back in the snow and mountains."

Narcissa was burdened almost beyond human endurance with work and responsibility. But what could one do? She took the sufferers all into her great lonely heart and made their sorrows her own.

Among the strangers that came to the mission door was a gaunt consumptive. "The Pacific fog will do you no good," said the doctor after looking him over. "You turn in here."

This man, Joseph Findlay, had been a Mississippi pilot until the wasting malady had stricken him and he had sought healing in the mountain air of the West. After the children were put to bed Narcissa would sit by his bedside until midnight. Her simple faith in the things of the spirit brought a wonderful sense of spiritual light and peace to the dying man.

"I am overprivileged," he said calmly, "to die in such a quiet place."

GATHERING STORM

The Indians of the upper Columbia watched the passing wagon trains with gloomy forebodings.

Whitman too realized how certain it was that the oncoming immigration would destroy whatever stood in its way. With their backs against the Pacific Ocean, the Indians could make no further retreat. It seemed certain that the two forces must come to a final and violent collision.

Some of the Indians were profiting from this situation.

They rode as far as Fort Hall to meet the immigrant trains and traded fresh horses for the exhausted animals of the pioneers at the rate of five or six fagged horses for one fresh one. The Indians grazed these worn animals for a few months until they were in good condition and again traded them for worn-out horses.

In the Grande Ronde the Cayuses were listening to an Indian prophet urging them to destroy the white invaders who were coming to take their land. He was an educated Delaware Indian named Tom Hill. He was traveling among the Western tribes and by his powerful eloquence was stirring up the Indians to unite and resist the pale-faced invaders who were relentlessly driving them into the Western Ocean.

Another cause for uneasiness was the code of laws which Elijah White had drawn up and was urging on the unwilling Indians. The tribes around the Waiilatpu Mission were fiercely divided between those who had adopted the white man's teaching and ways, and those who clung to their tribal customs and were determined to hold their lands against the white immigrants.

The Nez Percés, the Walla Wallas, and the Cayuses had met in council. The Indians had not enough cattle for the winter. They organized a band under Elijah, son of the Walla Walla chief Peu-peu-mox-mox, the Yellow Serpent, to go to Spanish California and purchase cattle. The Indians bargained with the Spaniards for their cattle and started home with the herd. On the way they had a run in with a band of Indian horse thieves. In the ensuing fight Elijah's band not only beat the horse thieves but captured their horses. Unfortunately these had been stolen from the whites. When some of the white men from Sutter's Fort tried to claim their animals Elijah refused to surrender them, as his braves had taken them from an enemy in a fair fight.

Being a devout Christian, Elijah went with four of his braves to Sutter's Fort to attend the Sabbath services. Afterward the white men at the fort had taken him into an adjoining room and told him that he was condemned to die. Elijah asked to be allowed to pray. He turned his back and kneeled down. A white man stepped behind him and shot him dead. This brutal outrage stirred all the tribes of the Columbia Valley to anger. The crime called for vengeance. A tribal council was held, with Whitman and Spalding present, to discuss whether a white chief—preferably Whitman—should die to avenge Elijah's murder. No decision was reached. One brave accused Marcus of being a poisoner and sorcerer, and another threatened Spalding with torture and death. But in spite of this the Christian Indians were friendly and willing to work with Marcus.

"Notwithstanding all these discouragements we do not think we are authorized to feel we are in danger so as to warrant us to leave our post at present," wrote Whitman.

"ALL OR NONE," WINTER, 1844–1845

One day in early October the mission was roused by rifle fire and shouting. Three dusty horsemen rode in, whooping and waving their hats. These were the outriders of the annual immigration. Another wagon train was soon to arrive.

Marcus had been expecting it and was prepared. The grain bins were full and the cattle herd was fat and strong. "Reckon there must be close to three hundred wagons behind us," said a scout. "I'd figger there was nigh on fifteen hundred persons all told. They are strung out all the way from here to Powder River, and most of 'em ain't got over the Blue Mountains yet. If they don't make it soon they'll be runnin' into snow for sure. Most of 'em will be headin' on down the Umatilla to the Dalles," he added.

"Here's a rifle I'm leaving with you. It will be called for later," said the leader as he rode away.

For those who could pay, Marcus had flour at six dollars for a hundred pounds (the immigrants had paid twelve dollars at Laramie), and beef on the hoof at six cents a pound. This traffic kept the mission self-supporting.

Mr. Greene wrote: "We are not quite sure that you ought to devote so much time and thought to feeding the emigrants, and thus make your station a great restaurant for the weary pilgrims on their way to their promised land."

Marcus replied: "If we are not legally, religiously, or morally bound to relieve the passing Emigrant we are necessarily; for the sick and hungry cannot be sent away however penniless. The wants of those who have no money are equally pressing, for they are the wants of hunger."

The wagons were now beginning to arrive. Unshaven men in patched and tattered clothes and worn boots, tired women in dusty skirts and sunbonnets, dirty-faced children, lousy, unwashed, and barefooted. Narcissa assigned each family camping space, or quarters in the Emigrant House—for the sick. A great scrubbing of children and washing of clothes began at once.

A ramshackle wagon drew up at the mission door. Narcissa went out and said to the miserable-looking boy who sat on the driver's box, "Who are you, and where are your folks?"

"I'm John Sager and I'm fourteen years old, ma'am. This is my brother Francis. He's twelve." He turned and revealed a towheaded boy behind him. "Our folks is dead, ma'am," he added miserably. "They died back on the trail."

"Any more of you?" asked Narcissa.

"Yes'm. We got five sisters, and one is the baby."

"Where are they?" asked Narcissa.

"Cathy, Liza, Louisa, Mat," called the boy.

Down from the tailboard climbed the four little girls. Catherine, the oldest, limped badly. "The wagon ran over her leg," said the boy.

An old woman appeared with a bundle in her arms. "This is the baby," she said. "Five months old. It's a sad story, ma'am."

In a few minutes Narcissa was washing and feeding the baby. The six older children were scrubbed, deloused, clothed, and fed.

"Here's your new family," called Narcissa to Marcus as he came in that evening. He was surprised to meet the large addition to the family, but agreed to Narcissa's plea to adopt them all—except, he said, the baby. He thought that would be too heavy a responsibility for her.

"All or none," said Narcissa very positively. "All or none, Marcus. I want her as a kind of charm to bind the others to me," she added wistfully.

They were like wolf cubs at first, savage and untamed. With her patience, wisdom, and love, Narcissa "subdued" them, as she called it, until they were a friendly, obedient, and very lively family of youngsters. Like the rest of the mission, they began the day with a plunge into the river, summer and winter. Among the girls there was a great yearning for dolls. Narcissa contrived several rag creatures and marked their faces in pen and ink. They were not very lifelike, but they served perfectly for the imaginations of the restless little girls.

In a corner John Sager found a rifle. On the butt the initials H. S. were carved. Excitedly he called his brother and sisters. "It's Dad's rifle. Look!" He pointed to the crudely cut initials.

"Yes," said Marcus, "it was left here by a stranger who said it would be called for." The children all agreed that it should be John Sager's because he was the oldest. It would be a family heirloom that they would always cherish.

Narcissa now had eleven children. There were the seven Sagers, David Malin, Mary Anne Bridger, Helen Meek, and Perrin Whitman. In addition to the children, there were the men who worked for Marcus, and perhaps a dozen families now living at the so-called Emigrant House and in the tool house. Besides feeding these, the mission had to take care of the children's school, the Indians' school, and regular church services. Marcus and Narcissa shared in these arduous duties.

Besides attending to the farming and cattle, the grist-mill and the sawmill, Marcus answered all medical calls within a radius of two hundred miles, settled or averted the Indian difficulties that were perpetually arising, and carried on a correspondence with the American Board, giving full reports of current activities.

ANDREW RODGERS

Among the strangers who came to the mission door from over the mountains, young Mr. Andrew Rodgers arrived from Monmouth, Illinois. Narcissa wrote of him:

The Lord has sent us a dear good brother who has now been with us more than a year, in whose society I find much enjoyment and satisfaction. We talk, sing, labor and study together; indeed, he is the best associate I ever had, Marcus excepted, and better than I ever expect to get again.

Andrew had been a Seceder but, under the influence of Narcissa, had seen the light and joined the mission church. He was a good teacher for children, sang and played the violin. He caught the crusading spirit of the mission and began to study for the ministry. He went among the Indians and learned their language, and—which took more courage—he tackled Greek and Hebrew.

On occasion he wrote sermons on discouraging subjects and delivered them at Sunday services.

Yesterday was the Sabbath and to us all it was an interesting day. We are blessed as we have not been before in many years. We feel that we now enjoy in a great measure the labor of a minister. Brother Rodgers you know is pursuing a course of study with a view to that calling. He frequently writes a dissertation upon some theological subject and reads it to us on Sabbath. Last evening he gave us an extemporaneous discourse upon the future punishment of the wicked. It was truly edifying.

This was very high praise from Narcissa.

Henrietta, the youngest of the Sagers, could now navigate boldly on two legs and talk baby talk. She was full of mischief and tried to bully her foster parents.

Henrietta, my baby, is a sweet, interesting child, and loves me as my own Alice used to, and I love her dearly; but that tender anxiety so peculiar to mothers for their own offspring, is not for me to feel toward her, because it is impossible. She is now two years and five months old, and attends school and is very happy.

In recent years the crops had been bountiful and the gristmill was daily grinding out sacks of the precious white dust. Marcus knew that the strong and well-provided immigrants would keep to the Umatilla and reach the Dalles, where they could go on down the Columbia in bateaux to the Willamette. But it was the sick, the broken, and the starving who needed his help when they stumbled into Waiilatpu because they could go no farther. It was three hundred miles to the Willamette valley.

Looking forward, Marcus was planning for schools. There was the need for books, food for the mind. He had made out a list of books which he begged Mr. Greene to send. Sooner or later there would be a college—perhaps not so far off; the Dalles would be a good location. He wanted to keep abreast of the times in his profession too. He needed reference books and medical books. There was need for books on religion and the Bible. Latin, Greek, and Hebrew grammars, and Bible concordances, were needed for young men wanting to study for the ministry.

The autumn of 1847 the crops were poorer than usual, and Marcus had heard reports that the immigration would be heavier this year. A new road had been opened through to the Cascade Mountains, called the Barlow Road or "the cut-off around Mount Hood." Marcus hoped this might take care of most of the immigrant traffic. He had a lame knee from a horse fall and wanted to give up heavy work and devote all his time and strength to teaching the Indians.

Instead he took two wagons down to the Dalles and back, breaking a new road that was shorter and through grass country. One great advantage of the new road was that it ran far back from the Columbia. The river Indians had preyed upon the passing immigrants, stealing horses and cattle. Coming back along the shores of the Columbia, Marcus demanded from them the return of all stolen property. The Indians willingly returned it, so great was his influence among them. He warned them that any further pilfering would mean that the Americans would certainly come and recover their property and punish the thieves.

In his letters to Greene, Marcus pleaded for more settlers for Oregon. He wrote detailed instructions to pioneers for making the trip, urging the secretary to spread the news about Oregon all over New England:

Can a mind be found so narrow as not to be willing to part with a Pastor; or a Pastor not to part with a church member; simply because they are good men and useful where they are?

Mr. Greene was only speaking for New England, for Beacon Hill and the comfortable and satisfied East, when he replied:

That families who are well off and doing well here will go there [to Oregon] simultaneously, for that purpose, I have no expectation or belief; nor do I think the Providence of God calls them to do it.

On this point I am so doubtful that I should be unwilling to endeavor to persuade any family to do it, or even young men without families, unless there was evidence of their moral principles and Christian character.

HOPES AND PLANS

Narcissa was the calm, wise head of the teeming but ordered life of the mission. The years of heavy physical labor were over for her, as there were now children and women to carry out the daily domestic routines. She loved to preside quietly at the children's singing and sewing meetings and the long table that accommodated twenty. The mission was always full of children. She lived for the children. She loved to sing with them, and her voice was still clear and sweet.

She watched with admiration and anxiety the tireless labors of Marcus on large and forward-reaching plans for the new world that was pouring into the wilderness each year to make a great new state. He was busy with crops, plows, a new Indian school, the beginnings of a college, a memorial to Congress to establish a line of posts to Oregon. In this last he outlined a plan for a pony express: "The mail may, with a change of horses at every fifty miles, be carried at the rate of from one hundred to one hundred and fifty miles in twenty-four hours." His plans were always practical, and he was the first to take action on them.

Narcissa wrote of him:

He is all benevolence, has amazing energy of thought and action, nothing is too hard or impossible for him to do, that can be done. I often think he cannot last always; indeed, his strength is not what it used to be, although his health is quite good.

A head and heart more full of benevolent plans, and hands more ready in the execution of them for the good of the poor Indian and the white population of the country, you have probably never seen.

The immigrants' trains passing by each fall had revived a long-cherished hope in her heart. "Kala tilapsa kunku" ("I am longing for you continually to sing with") she wrote to her sister Jane. She urged Jane to come to Oregon. In her dream she saw all her brothers and sisters coming to Oregon. Why not? The way across the prairie and mountains was open now to the beautiful valley of the Columbia. The grassy acres were waiting for flocks of sheep, the mild seasons made it possible for the cattle to range all winter, the fertile soil was ready for the plow, for orchards. She was sure her parents would come too. They would all be together again in the promised land.

WOLF SONG

The little yellow squares of light in the mission windows shone in the vast wilderness darkness. A lone wolf howl rose and hung in the night, a wail of desolation and despair.

Gazing into the ember glow of the fire, the doctor thought of his sheep. He had seventy-two of them. There would have been more if it had not been for the raiding wolves. He had left pieces of poisoned meat about the sheep pens. Occasionally he found the stiff carcass of a dead wolf in the neighborhood, so he knew the poison worked. Sometimes an Indian had picked up the meat and dropped it into the family pot. The results had been disturbing.

But it was not the wolves that had raided Mr. Gray's melon patch. He had dosed some of the riper fruit with a strong cathartic, and there had been violent interior disturbances in the tepees of the Cayuse camp.

A growing rumor spread among the tribes that the doctor was a sorcerer and poisoner. Joe Lewis, the halfbreed hanger-on, and Tamsuky, called the Murderer, fanned the legend among the Indians around the campfires. There were other things that troubled the spirit of the Cayuses as they darkly watched the immigrant wagons that now rolled on by the hundreds toward the Willamette valley. Each year the wagons came in greater numbers. Soon the whites would take away the Indians' land. A vast uneasiness and prophetic foreboding possessed the minds of the Indians along the trail.

The measles had come over the Blue Mountains with the wagons and was spreading among the Indian villages. The measles were a very minor plague with the whites, compared to the cholera, but among the Indians the contagion spread terror, and fear spread death. Whole families lay dying in the filth and fetid air of the lodges. It was plainly the work of the evil spirits loosed against them by the white sorcerers.

The ancient law of the tribes called for vengeance on their destroyers.

A VISIT FROM MR. SPALDING

The emigration of '47 had passed. Endlessly the great white tops had creaked and rumbled down the Umatilla, bringing four thousand more settlers to Oregon. The Willamette country now had some ten thousand white American settlers. Soon many of these would advance up the Columbia to settle the rich lands of the Walla Walla and Cayuse Indians.

Marcus was bringing the machinery for his new gristmill up the river from the Dalles. The great migrations needed more and more flour as they poured down from the Blue Mountains. Whitman was pleased that the Indians about the mission, who had learned to plow and hoe, seemed to cling more obediently and willingly to the white man's protection. At Waiilatpu there was peace and more cooperation from the Christian Indians than ever before.

Halfway down the great waterway of the Columbia, near the Dalles, the Methodists had conducted their mission at Waskopum. It was of great strategic importance in the mission work, for here the Indians of the coast and interior met annually for trade. When Marcus heard that the Methodists intended to abandon this post he at once proposed to take over the mission and persuaded the Board to purchase it. Although this meant increased work and responsibility, he felt the project to be vitally important to the success of the work among the Indians.

Perrin Whitman and Mr. A. Hinman, who had taught

at Waiilatpu, were sent to take charge of the work at Waspopum. Marcus planned to start new schools here and, some day, a college.

One mild day in the latter part of November, Mr. Spalding rode into the mission from Lapwai, at the head of a pack train of horses loaded with grain to be ground in the gristmill. With him was his ten-year-old daughter Eliza. She had come to attend the mission school. The mission girls were all excited about having Eliza as guest for the winter and were making plans for good times.

After a pleasant chat with the doctor, Spalding and Andrew Rodgers continued on for a visit at Fort Walla Walla. That night they stopped at the village of the famous chief Peu-peu-mox-mox. He was the father of the murdered Elijah, and his heart was again saddened, for that night another member of his family died from a sudden illness. Next morning the two white men accompanied the funeral procession to the Indian burial ground below Fort Walla Walla. Mr. Spalding read the service and continued on to the fort. Here they met the Reverend Father Brouillet, who had been appointed Catholic bishop at Walla Walla. Next day was Mr. Spalding's forty-fourth birthday. After an agreeable dinner, at which these clergymen of different faiths expressed cordial good will, Spalding and Rodgers rode back to Waiilatpu.

THE WARNING

Whitman and Spalding rode through the dark and in rain and mud on the familiar trail that led from Waiilatpu to the Umatilla thirty miles away. The doctor was answering

the call of Young Chief to come and heal the stricken people of his village on the Umatilla. Spalding had agreed to
accompany him.

At times the two men talked to each other in the darkness. It had been eleven years since they had first followed
this trail—crowded years that seemed a century. The ri-
valries and strife that had flared up so often had faded out.
Reconciliations with reconsecration to the noble purposes
of their work had healed the old bitterness. Each had held
a light in the darkness and kept the faith against grim odds,
risking life and giving all. Now the work was nearly done.
With the country settled there would be no need for the
missions.

As the dawn broke they came out on a clearing by the
river. Here was the lodge of Istakus. The old savage was
wise and subtle as a snake. He seemed the most pious of
all the Christian Indians but behind his impassive face
lurked the savage impulses of his race. With his squaw,
children, and dogs, he welcomed the white men. They sat
in a friendly circle and had breakfast.

After breakfast Whitman mounted his horse and rode
on alone, across the river and for some six miles, to Young
Chief's village.

He spent a day of grim doctor's business in the dark
tepees of the Cayuses. He gave what medicines he had and
strove to rouse the stricken from the despair and primitive
resignation to death that was more fatal than the malady
itself.

Here Marcus learned that the Reverend Father Brouillet
and his assistant had yesterday occupied the house of
Young Chief. At the end of the day he briefly visited the

two priests, and found Mr. Spalding with them. The doctor wanted to reach home that night and so refused an invitation to stop for supper. He cordially urged the two priests to visit the mission at Waiilatpu.

As he rode past Istakus's lodge the old Indian came out and hailed him. He had bad news. Tamsuky, the Murderer, was telling the Indians that the doctor was destroying them by sorcery, and he, Tamsuky, had said he was going to kill the doctor. Istakus spoke the truth, let the doctor take warning. Marcus had heard this threat so often before that he put it down as merely the gossip of the garrulous old savage and hurried off. If he made haste he would be home in six hours.

It was after ten at night when the weary doctor turned his faithful horse out on the range and entered the warm and glowing room. "Go to bed, lads. I will take over from here on," he said.

The two Sager boys had been watching by the bedsides of Catherine and Louise Sager and Helen Mar Meek. They were all ill, and Helen and Louise were in a serious condition. For a long time the doctor sat beside the wasted form of little Helen Meek. Presently he arose and came and sat beside Narcissa. Taking her hand, he said sadly, "Helen is sinking rapidly. She doesn't seem to respond. I do not think she can live."

For a long while they talked. Their plans for helping the Cayuses were darkened by the dreadful scourge of measles that was ravaging the Indian tribes as far as Fort Hall. Narcissa said that when a child of one of the settlers had died of the measles she had shown the body to the Indians to prove that the whites too died of the plague. But this had no effect on the Indians' resentment. Marcus mentioned the threat that Istakus had reported. They could only go on as they had done, serving white immigrant and stricken Indian alike as best they knew.

THE BLOW FALLS, NOVEMBER 29, 1847

Monday morning Marcus rose early as usual. As Narcissa had not come down from her room he cheerfully made breakfast and sent Eliza up with a tray of food for Narcissa. When she came down the little girl said that "Mother" was weeping and would not eat. Marcus understood. Pioneer women had their own private Gethsemanes, which they could only go through alone. He was soon absorbed in the crowding duties of the mission. The ringing of the blacksmith's anvil, the monotonous grinding of the millstones, the carpenter's hammer, told that the mission was starting another busy week. When the doctor came in at noon Narcissa gave him her usual cheery greeting. Marcus had just come from the cemetery, where he had read the funeral service for an Indian child who had succumbed to the measles.

That afternoon, after attending to several patients about the mission, the doctor came into the living room, where Narcissa was bathing the children, and sat down. In the kitchen John Sager, weak from a recent illness, sat twisting broom cord as he talked to little Mary Anne Bridger, who was washing the dinner dishes.

There was a sudden commotion at the kitchen door, and

Mary went to open it. Two Indians stepped boldly into the room wrapped in blankets. She recognized Chief Tilau-kaik, and behind him the grim visage of Tamsuky.

"Me sick. Want medicine from doctor," he said roughly, pushing the child aside and pounding on the door to the living room. The doctor answered and, seeing the Indians, stepped into the kitchen, closing the door behind him. Narcissa went to the door, listened a moment, and then went to the living-room stove with the four-year-old Henrietta in her arms. From the adjoining "Indian" room, where her family lived, Mrs. Osborne appeared, closing the door behind her.

Suddenly the report of a rifle in the kitchen blasted the air. For a moment everyone in the living room stood frozen. Suddenly Mary Anne burst into the room, screaming, "Father and John! The Indians have killed them! Tamsuky struck Father from behind with his ax, and Tilaukaik shot John!"

The children joined in Mary Anne's frightened screams and ran for the door. Narcissa walked to the bed, laid Henrietta down, and carefully covered her with a blanket.

"You children come back here and put your clothes on," she called sharply. Tremblingly they came back and began putting on their clothes.

"Mrs. Osborne, go back to your room and lock the door," Narcissa said calmly to the other woman. For an instant she paused before the kitchen door and then firmly pushed it open.

On the bloodstained floor, by an overturned chair, lay the two bodies. As she took Marcus in her arms she wailed, "What can I do? Is there anything I can do?"

"No," came faintly from the lips of the stricken man.

At this moment a man bolted into the living room, shouting wildly, "The Indians are killing us all." He sank to the floor, holding his wounded arm. "Water," he gasped hoarsely.

Narcissa moved swiftly, her white face set. She placed a pitcher of water by the wounded man, locked all the doors, and returned to the kitchen. As she tried to lift Marcus by his shoulders, two distracted women came in. Together they moved Marcus into the sitting room and laid him on the floor near the bed.

Outside the Mission House

Outside the Emigrant House hung the huge carcass of a freshly slaughtered beef. Three men were cutting it into quarters with an ax. A group of Indians hung about idly, watching the white men at work. There were more of them than usual, all wrapped in the familiar blankets.

At the shot from the mission house, these Indians sprang into action. Throwing off their blankets, they opened up with the guns they had been concealing. At the first volley one man was hit in the arm. He turned and ran for the mission.

Another, Canfield the carpenter, grazed by a bullet, ran for his shop. Here he caught up his youngest child, called on his three other children to follow, and dashed for the Emigrant House, which they all reached in safety.

The man with the ax was unhurt. "Come on, you red devils, come on," he yelled, swinging the ax in short circles. A dozen Indians with knives and tomahawks milled around him. He stood with his back against the red carcass of the beef, maneuvering the ax with a deadly skill that held off the circling pack. As he struck again and again, he muttered a sort of death chant to himself: "Come on, you varmints, I'll show you." At every rush of the savages he swung the ax in a short arc that swept back his enemies.

Finally an Indian sprang in behind the beef carcass and stuck his knife into the man's back.

At the mission house the teacher in the schoolroom, at the sound of the first shot, concealed the children in a sort of gallery adjoining it and engaged in a desperate hand-to-hand fight with two Indians armed with knives. Another white man was fatally stabbed while climbing a fence. The tailor was mortally shot from the door of his shop. An agile carpenter escaped the attackers and started for Fort Walla Walla, reaching there in safety with first news of disaster.

Andrew Rodgers was working in the garden, some thirty yards from the mission house. When the firing began he bolted for the door of the mission, which Narcissa had locked. He threw himself against it, breaking the two panes of glass. Narcissa stepped to the door, unbolted it, and let the frantic young man in. Before she could close the door a bullet struck her in the shoulder, and she sank to the floor.

Rodgers, holding his wounded wrist, saw the doctor lying on the floor. "Is he dead?" he asked in a horrified whisper.

"No," came from the lips of the prostrate form.

Clinging to Narcissa in the mission house were the five Sager girls, Helen Mar Meek, and Mary Anne Bridger. Helen and Louise were seriously ill. Besides these there were three women and two wounded men. On the floor lay the doctor; at times he seemed to be half conscious. Behind the locked door of the Indian room were the five members of the Osborne family. John Osborne was an intelligent mechanic who worked for the mission. His wife had not fully recovered from a recent illness. With them were their three children, aged five, seven, and nine.

With frontier ingenuity for self-preservation, Osborne took up the floorboards, concealed the family and himself beneath them, and carefully replaced the flooring.

IN THE SITTING ROOM

The women helped Narcissa to her feet. She was bleeding badly from the shoulder wound. This was the end of the song. This was the last sacrifice. Her life had been one long sacrifice; she was used to it. One thing filled her mind— save the children. "God spare the children," she prayed. Then, "Everyone upstairs," she ordered.

It was rapidly growing dark. The children were marshaled quietly up the stairs. The sick girls were laid on the floor. In a few moments there was a shattering of glass, as a window was smashed below stairs, and the sound of an ax crashing in doors. Suddenly the lower room was filled with yelling Indians. One gashed the doctor's face with his ax, others were mutilating the body of John Sager. The looting began.

Presently an Indian advanced cautiously toward the stairs. It was Tamsuky, the Murderer. In the darkness above, the barrel of a rifle was thrust forward. The Indian stopped. In a whining voice he said he wanted to save the women and children. The killing was over, but the Indians were preparing to burn the house. If the women and children would come down he would conduct them to safety in the Emigrant House.

It was a desperate choice between death by fire or by Indian hatchets. There was a faint hope that, if Tamsuky was speaking the truth, they would be spared. In the dark his promises were repeated in a coaxing voice.

Finally Narcissa called, "We will come."

Very slowly she came down the stairs, step by step, leaning heavily against Rodgers. At her feet, as she entered the sitting room, lay the body of Marcus. Dimly she could see his mangled face. Her knees gave way, and she sank to the floor. Rodgers lifted and carried her across the room and laid her on the settee. "Bring the children's clothing," she ordered. The women laid the garments on the bloodstained sofa where she lay. "Let us go," she said faintly.

Joe Lewis and Rodgers picked up the settee between them and carried it through the kitchen and out the door. In the kitchen were the schoolchildren, who had been called in from the upper gallery of the schoolroom where they had been hiding. Francis Sager was the oldest among them, and an Indian seized him and pushed him out the door ahead of the settee.

Ten feet beyond the door Joe Lewis dropped his end of the settee and ran. A volley of shots rang out. Francis Sager fell with a bullet in his chest.

Rodgers dropped the settee and fell, fatally wounded. The body of Narcissa rolled in the mud. She had received two bullets in her breast. An Indian stepped forward, seized her by the hair, and lashed her face savagely with his riding whip.

Inside the mission house a wounded man and seven children lay on the floor of the attic in the darkness.

After the murders outside the kitchen door the Indians had left. They believed that in the night the spirits of the murdered came seeking vengeance on their destroyers.

In the Emigrant House the Indians had now collected forty women and children. In the mission attic the sick girls whimpered for water. The wounded man brought up a pitcherful. They found that the water was dark with blood. It was too horrible to drink. The clock struck the hours with an awful sound of doom. There were noises in the darkness below. Finally all fell into an uneasy sleep.

OSBORNE'S STORY

Under the floor in the Indian room Mrs. Osborne weakly held her children close. Beside her John Osborne lay listening. "We lay there listening to the firing—the screams of women and children—the groans of the dying—not knowing how soon our turn would come. We were however not discovered." After the last volley they could hear someone groaning far into the night. Then it was still for a long time.

"Now," whispered Osborne, "we must start for the fort. It is our only chance. If we wait here until morning they will find us." Carefully he lifted the floorboards. All was still. He helped his wife to her feet, lifted the youngest on his back, took the seven-year-old on his arm. He opened the door softly and stepped out—into a pool of blood. Carefully they made their way among the mangled corpses and reached the woods. Mrs. Osborne was terribly weak. They had gone only two miles when day broke. They hid in a clump of bushes through the long day. Darkness came again, and they started on, but the woman was too weak to go far. Three miles farther on, Osborne concealed his wife and the two older children in the brush. "Don't move until I return," he said. He took the youngest on his back and started on through the dark. After twenty miles he sank down exhausted in the wet grass. When he woke the sun was high. He staggered on five miles farther and reached Fort Walla Walla.

McBean, the factor, treated him coldly, offered no assistance. But by night Osborne had found an Indian guide and two horses, and, with a little food, he started back. They hunted through the night but could find no trace of the family. Osborne gave up hope. In the morning the Indian guide again took up the quest. With his head bent forward he followed some invisible track through the thick undergrowth. Wearily Osborne kept on. Presently he heard the Indian calling. There they were, safe but weak and famished for food and water. Shortly the Indian appeared with a flask of water, and Osborne fed them bread. When they had gone two miles farther a strange Indian came riding up. He drew a pistol. For a moment it seemed that there would be another massacre. But Osborne's guide spoke fiercely to the enemy. There was a brief parley, and in a few minutes the Indian rode off.

"He says you must hurry or the mission Indians will find and murder you," said his guide.

By ten o'clock that night the exhausted family and the faithful Indian had reached the fort, where McBean allowed them to remain until they were able to return to Oregon City with the Ogden relief party.

"I can say little more about the massacre; we may say, however, that it was nothing but the hand of Almighty God, that delivered us out of the hand of these cruel savages," concluded Mr. Osborne gratefully as he finished his story.*

The women and the children in the Emigrant House were fed and guarded by the Indians. They would be useful when it came to squaring accounts with the Americans.

The mission house was stripped, and the murderers quarreled over the loot. A young man driving a wagon in from the sawmill was waylaid and killed. Two white families were brought down from the sawmill by the Indians and forced to operate the gristmill to provide food for the captives.

Two sick white men were found and clubbed to death by the Indians as they lay in bed. In a few days the children Louise Sager and Helen Mar Meek, who had been so desperately ill, died.

Tuesday evening Father Brouillet arrived at the mission. Shaken by the gory scene and the sight of the wretched captives, he spent a dismal night by the Indian campfires. Next day the mangled bodies of Marcus and Narcissa were laid side by side with eight other victims in a shallow common grave. Fourteen whites had been massacred.

The tall priest in his black robe read the Catholic burial service at the grave. These were not of his flock, but it was not the time or place to make distinctions.

* Quoted in Archer and Dorothy Hulbert, *Marcus Whitman, Crusader*. Colorado Springs: The Stewart Commission of Colorado College: 1936–41.

It was soon evident to Father Brouillet that the Indians were planning to murder Spalding on his arrival at Waiilatpu. If his life was to be saved, the priest realized, he must warn him. He determined to ride toward the Umatilla in the hope of meeting Spalding on the way.

Just before he left, Edward, the son of Chief Tilaukaik, announced he would accompany Father Brouillet and bring the news of the massacre to the Indian camp on the Umatilla. The priest realized that this meant another hazard for Spalding.

As they came up the trail from the river, Brouillet saw a man riding toward them, driving several horses ahead of him. It was Spalding. The priest quickly turned to the interpreter and said, "Tell Edward I ask him as a special favor to spare this man's life." Edward looked very doubtful and replied, "I am not a chief, I cannot take it upon myself to save him. I will ride back to the mission and consult my people. I will come back and let you know," he added as he turned back on the trail and rode away.

Spalding's first inquiry was for news of the mission. The priest hurriedly told him the grim story, warning him that the Indians were seeking to kill him, and that if he didn't escape before Edward returned it probably meant death.

"What shall I do?" moaned Spalding.

"I have warned you. It's now up to you," Brouillet replied. "You must act quickly. The mission is only three miles away, and the Cayuses will be here soon."

Spalding turned his spare horses over to the interpreter. He thanked the priest and bade him farewell. The interpreter showed him the trail and told him a safe route to Lapwai. Spalding rode off in the gathering dusk.

Within twenty minutes Edward and three braves rode up angrily. They accused the priest of interfering and aiding Spalding's escape. They dashed on down the trail Spalding had taken. It was growing dark, and the heavy evening fog drifted in, obscuring everything.

The Indians soon gave up the pursuit, as the trail was lost in the fog and darkness. The priest rode on, praying for Spalding's safety.

Spalding, traveling by night on roundabout trails, reached Lapwai in safety after six days, starving and exhausted. He and his family took refuge with an old mountain man against the wrath of Nez Percés, and were later ransomed by Peter Skene Ogden.

McBean, the factor at Fort Walla Walla, immediately sent news of the massacre to Fort Vancouver. In ten days Peter Skene Ogden, a Canadian fur trader, and his party arrived at Walla Walla with two barges. He called the Cayuses to a council and bought back the survivors, including the Spaldings, for shirts and guns, and took them all safely down the river to Fort Vancouver.

The Cayuses burned the mission at Waiilatpu and disappeared into the wilderness. Months later, when American soldiers came, they found the victims' grave but wolves and coyotes had dug up the bodies of the massacred. The soldiers buried what was left in a deeper grave under wagon beds on higher ground.

None of the murderers were captured, but later five Indians gave themselves up at Oregon City. When they were asked why they gave themselves up, one of them said, "Christ died for the people. We will die for our people." They were tried, sentenced, and hanged.

For many years the State of Oregon prohibited settle-ment in the Walla Walla country because of Indian "troubles." The rain and sun and fog of the slow years passed over the unmarked graves at Waiilatpu. The dirt mound sank until it was almost effaced in the grass of the level prairie. Those who remembered came and marked the place with a rough fence. Then students of Whitman College reverently built a paling around the spot.

The herds multiplied on the thousand hills of Oregon, the wheat and the corn sprang up in green and golden abun-dance, and in the great orchards the heavy fruit weighed the bending branches to the ground. The sons and daugh-ters of the pioneers of the Oregon Trail fashioned the free institutions of a great new state.

To the shores of the Pacific, churches, schools, libraries spread the light of mind and spirit among the free people.

The dream of the marchers of the Oregon Trail, the pioneers, the trail-breakers, the dream of Marcus and Narcissa Whitman and the others asleep under the prairie sod by the Walla Walla, has come true in splendid and enduring reality.

EPILOGUE

Among the some thirty Cayuses who took part in the massacre there were devout Christian Indians, and some had received many kindnesses from the Whitmans. The massacre was not so much an act of personal hatred and vengeance as the last desperate retaliation of a doomed people against their destroyers. For two hundred years the Indians had been driven relentlessly westward until there was nothing between them and the Pacific Ocean.

The fate of the mission between these ruthless forces was inevitable. The tragedy of the Whitmans was determined from the beginning, by their uncompromising idealism and by the forces of history. At times they were acutely aware that this was so.

Of the seventy-two persons at or near the mission at the time of the massacre, forty-two were children. It is significant that none of them except the two Sager boys were harmed by the Indians. Of the fourteen people murdered, only one was a woman. Considering the desperate mood of the Indians of the whole region, and the deliberately unprotected state of the mission, it is surprising that so few were killed.

To the Whitmans, being what they were, any other course of action than the one they chose was unthinkable. They were dedicated to a Christian mission. Of what they had to give they gave all to the very end, asking for themselves nothing.

There have not been many like them, but there have been enough. Their names are not written large in the history books, but they are not forgotten and will never be. There have been some others of their kind, before them and after. The survivors of the first winter at Plymouth Plantation would have understood the Whitmans' story. It was what they would have expected of their children.